Biografeats

Life Lessons of Courage, Perseverance, and Triumph

RICHARD LAM

ILLUSTRATIONS BY BRYAN KOTWICA

iUniverse, Inc.
New York   Bloomington

Biografeats
Life Lessons of Courage, Perseverance, and Triumph

Copyright © 2009 Richard Lam

iUniverse books may be ordered through booksellers or by contacting:

iUniverse
1663 Liberty Drive
Bloomington, IN 47403
www.iuniverse.com
1-800-Authors (1-800-288-4677)

ISBN: 978-1-4401-4874-3 (pbk)
ISBN: 978-1-4401-4873-6 (cloth)
ISBN: 978-1-4401-4875-0 (ebk)

Printed in the United States of America

iUniverse rev. date: 6/30/2009

Illustrations by Bryan Kotwica

For Mom, Dad, and Grandma

I am tired of waiting for Destiny.
Destiny will just have to wait for me.
Richard Lam

Contents

Preface..ix
Acknowledgments xi
Introduction...xiii

1. Change the World...1
2. The Young Man and the Sea 10
3. Shooting Star 19
4. Peace by Peace...27
5. Iron Will...37
6. Dreams Do Come True.. 46
7. The Pursuit of Happiness 55
8. Al Mighty 63
9. Heart of Gold...72
10. Stand and Deliver...80
11. Have No Fear..88
12. Follow Your Passion 99
13. Never Stop Learning 108
14. Golden Opportunities... 118
15. No Matter What They Say 128
16. Climb as High as You Can...138
17. Always Be Curious 147
18. Rebel with a Cause 156
19. You Never Know..166
20. It Was All Worth It 173
21. Never Out of Style 181
22. Freedom Fighter..190
23. Dare to Soar.. 200
24. Mr. Perseverance 210

Endnotes..221
Bibliography...229

Preface

As a high school math teacher, I was constantly searching for ways to motivate my students. I wanted all of them to succeed, not only in my math class but also in life. To motivate them, I would regularly stress the importance of hard work, a positive mental attitude, and a strong sense of self-belief by sharing inspirational stories with them. But I didn't know that many stories the students could relate to. One night in early November 2007, I came upon an idea that I thought would inspire students to be more diligent and perhaps inspire them to reach their limitless potential one day.

Since my teenage years, I've enjoyed reading biographies and autobiographies of people who achieved a great deal of success. What I enjoyed most from reading these books were the life lessons these individuals offered. The lessons I learned helped me succeed in life. I thought that if students were exposed to more inspiring stories, such as the ones I read about, then maybe they could benefit like I did. So that's when I decided to write a book of mini-biographies based on truly inspirational lives from various backgrounds and cultures.

All of these stories are derived from published books. While the dialogues in each story are taken directly from sources that are cited, the composition of each story is original.

The purpose of this book is to inspire young readers as well as adults to achieve greater success by exposing them to life lessons from some of history's greatest achievers.

Acknowledgments

First, my appreciation goes to my parents for their unconditional love and support. I'm forever indebted to my mom for her sacrifice, for rescuing me from the reservoir, and for her timely inspirational words.

Second, a special thanks to Monita E. Var for suggesting that I write a book. Even though I laughed at her idea at the time, this book may never have been written if she had not planted the seed. To her husband, Lunal Khuon, my childhood friend who has helped and encouraged me to excel as we traveled parallel paths on our long road to success, thanks for making my travels more pleasant.

Next, special thanks go to my sister-in-law, Rezina Alam, and my sister, Mee Wai, for being my biggest fans from start to finish. And thanks to my brother Ray for offering to finance my book idea after reading just the first two stories in rough draft. Also, thanks to my sisters Mai May and May Ming for their support and valuable feedback on my stories.

Life would be less fulfilling without my dear friends Ingrid Cheung and Denny Lam. Thank you for being there in my good times and bad. You were the light at the end of my long, dark tunnel.

Thanks to my old friend Kai Sui Tse and his wife Po Yee Szeto for their support, loyalty, and generosity. Your friendship has enriched my life.

Thanks to Grace Zhang for her support and for recommending Bryan Kotwica, who did a superb job on the illustrations. Thanks, Bryan.

Finally, a heartfelt thanks to Min Yi Li for her love, encouragement, and brilliant ideas. Thank you for believing in me from the start.

Introduction

This book consists of twenty-four short biographies that are three to four pages in length. Each one of these stories you are about to read is based on an individual who found the courage to overcome great obstacles on his or her long road to success. These stories teach us that anyone can succeed in life and realize his or her dreams, regardless of culture, race, nationality, gender, and circumstance.

I deliberately chose twelve women and twelve men to give equal representation to both sexes.

The selection criteria for the individuals were based on several factors. First, I wanted people who achieved a high level of success. Second, I wanted individuals who have exemplified what I consider to be essential qualities in attaining success: courage, persistence, perseverance, sacrifice, desire, dreams, determination, diligence, attitude, and belief. Third, I wanted individuals from a wide array of backgrounds. There are artists, athletes, doctors, entertainers, entrepreneurs, humanitarians, inventors, lawyers, leaders, scientists, social activists, and teachers profiled in this book. Last, I wanted individuals from different cultures and different parts of the world. Individuals from eleven different countries are represented.

The stories are presented in an alternating manner, beginning with a story of a woman followed by a story of a man. Special care was given to the placement of the first and last story. I chose the first story because it is probably the least familiar to the majority of readers. The last story was chosen to give the reader a lasting impression of the person whose life has inspired me to persevere during my trying times and continues to inspire me to this day.

The arrangement of the stories follows the same format. Each one begins with the subject's childhood and then progresses through a course of events filled with challenges, adversities, failures, and successes, and finally ends with a major achievement. The identity of the individual is intentionally kept from the reader to make the reading more interesting. After the ending of each story, the reader is asked to determine the identity of the person behind the story. The page following this "test" question reveals the person's identity, along with a sketch of him or her. A separate page shows the subject's biographical information along with some more interesting facts about the subject. Finally, the last page shows a collection of selected quotes by the subject to help reveal more of the subject's character and beliefs.

This book is by no means a scholarly work. However, many hours of research have been devoted to the writing of this book. I hope you find these stories as informative and inspiring as I did.

CHANGE THE WORLD

There was just something about Maria. Once as a little girl, she watched in horror as her parents got into a big argument. Without saying a word, Maria took a chair and pulled it between them. She climbed on top of the chair and grabbed hold of her parents' hands as hard as she could. Peace was instantly restored in the home.

Maria continued with her helping ways. At the time, in the mid-1800s, Italy was an impoverished country where its citizens had little food or money. Since she came from a fairly well-off family, Maria was assigned to do a certain amount of knitting for the less fortunate every day. She made vests for babies, socks and scarves for men, and shawls for women to provide warmth. So, as a child, Maria learned the virtues of compassion and charity.

By nature, she was wise beyond her years. One time, Maria had fallen seriously ill and her worried mother stood by her bedside. The ten-year-old daughter calmly reassured her mother, "Don't worry, Mamma. I can't die," she said. "I have too much to do."[1] One thing Maria did not want to do was to take up teaching as a profession. Teaching never appealed to her because she saw how stressed teachers were. But at that time, teaching was the only profession open to women.

To give Maria the best education, her parents moved to Rome. She had always enjoyed mathematics. She figured that some day she would study engineering at the university. When her parents learned of her ambition, they were shocked. There were simply no schools for a girl to study advanced mathematics, let alone engineering. The only way Maria could study engineering would be to enroll in a boys' public school. So Maria's dad inquired at a number of schools, but each one of the principals refused to admit girls. Finally, one school agreed to accept her, but only under one condition: Maria could not cause any trouble for the boys or teachers.

1

After some time, Maria reconsidered and set her mind on studying medicine. Once again, she faced the same obstacle. Women were not admitted to medical school. But she just couldn't accept old tradition. So, father and daughter went to consult with Dr. Guido Bacelli, head of the board of education, but it was no use. Dr. Bacelli told Maria that it was impossible to study medicine at the University of Rome and advised her to choose a different career. Maria declined his advice. As she got up to leave the room, she looked calmly into Dr. Bacelli's eyes and confidently proclaimed, "I know I shall become a doctor of medicine."[2]

During the next few weeks, she bombarded the university authorities with her own letters and letters of recommendation from friends, relatives, and former teachers. Maria's persistence paid off. But life on the university campus was not easy. Some of the male students held outright resentment against her for being an intruder. Maria would retaliate against their gender discrimination. "Blow away. The harder you blow, the higher I go."[3]

During these difficult times, Maria's mom was her biggest supporter. In the evenings, Mom helped Maria memorize every little detail in the lecture notes. Maria's hard work eventually paid off. Her excellent grades won her a number of scholarships year after year. With the income from working as a private tutor, she managed to pay her way through college.

In 1896, Maria became the first woman doctor in Italy. Upon graduation, she was assigned to work at the psychiatric clinic at the University of Rome. Her first assignment was to visit the city's insane asylums and make observations. When she saw mentally retarded children for the first time, she was struck by the neglect of those young, lonely, miserable souls. These children, who were left to their own devices, would crawl on the floor looking for food crumbs.

After much observation, Maria felt that something could be done to help improve the lives of these children if only they had some sort of special teaching. But she didn't have any ideas. So she went to the library in search of information. There, she found a few books written by French doctors who had experimented with mentally retarded children and had produced some promising results. Further observation and research convinced her that these children needed education as much as normal children. Such an idea was revolutionary at the time. So she decided to give a series of lectures to raise public awareness and promote the idea of educating mentally retarded children.

Maria's eloquent speeches soon convinced the city officials to open the Orthophrenic School for children who were labeled as mentally deficient. Later on, the school opened their doors to children from insane asylums. When officials asked Maria to run the school, she accepted the challenge with enthusiasm. Each school day, she was there from 8 AM to 7 PM, teaching, observing, and experimenting with different teaching materials and methods. At night, she spent hours analyzing and reflecting on the day's work so that she could prepare new lesson plans for the next day.

For two years, Maria and her colleagues dedicated their lives to helping the children and developing an effective program for new teachers. She toured schools in London and Paris in search of better teaching methods. "Those two years of practice are indeed my first and only true degree in pedagogy,"[4] Maria recalled. Under her great leadership and teachings, the children made exceptional progress. She sent a group of her students to take the regular examinations that normal students took. Some of them performed better than the normal students! "Little by little," she said, "I became convinced that similar methods applied to normal children would develop and set free their personality in a marvelous and surprising way."[5] She embarked on a new mission.

In 1901, Maria left the Orthophrenic School and spent the next five years researching better methods of teaching normal children. Her research led to the discovery of significant works published by two French doctors, Dr. Edouard Seguin and Dr. Jean Itard. "I translated into Italian and copied out with my own hand the writing of these two men from beginning to end."[6] By the end of 1906, Maria finished her research project and was eager to test her new theories and methods on a class of normal children. But no school would allow her to test her unproven theories and methods. Maria would need to find pupils from somewhere else.

Then the perfect opportunity presented itself. To improve the lives of the children living in the notorious slum of San Lorenzo quarter in Rome, the city officials decided to open a daycare center in each of the tenement houses. These daycare centers, known as Children's Houses, were single rooms reserved for children who were six years old and under. Maria immediately seized the opportunity when she was asked to be the director for the Children's Houses. "I had," she said, "a strange feeling which made me announce emphatically that here was the opening of an undertaking of which the whole world would one day speak."[7]

First, she furnished the rooms with smaller furniture that fit the youngsters. Then she provided learning material that developed the children's senses, expanded their memories, and captured their attention. Within six months, these once-neglected children were learning at an astonishing rate. Word about Maria's miracle quickly spread throughout Rome and beyond. Soon, visitors from various places and backgrounds came to observe the children and study Maria's teaching principles. In just a few years, educators from around the world had adopted her revolutionary teaching ideas.

Who was this progressive teacher who changed the world of early childhood education?

MARIA MONTESSORI

Maria Montessori always had compassion for others. She dedicated her whole life to improving the lives and education of children. Her ideas changed the world.

MARIA MONTESSORI'S BIO

Birth Name: Maria Montessori
Birthplace: Chiaravalle, Italy
Birth Date: August 31, 1870
Died: May 6, 1952
Age: Eighty-one years old

ACHIEVEMENTS AND AWARDS

1904:   Professor of anthropology in the University of Rome

1913:   Conducted the First International Training Course

1914:   Established the American Montessori Society under the
        leadership of Alexander Graham Bell

1922:   Appointed the inspector of schools by the Italian
        government.

1925:   International Montessori Congress at Helsinki

1929:   Founded the Association Montessori Internationale in
        Amsterdam

1932:   International Montessori Congress in Europe

1939:   Brought her teaching ideas and methods to India

1949:   Nominated for the Nobel Peace Prize, again in 1951 and
        1952

Selected Quotes by Maria Montessori

"Children become like the things they love."

"Imitation is the first instinct of the awakening mind."

"Free the child's potential, and you will transform him into the world."

"The first essential for the child's development is concentration. The child who concentrates is immensely happy."

"Work is necessary; it can be nothing less than a passion; a person is happy in accomplishment."

"The greatest sign of success for a teacher is to be able to say, 'The children are now working as if I did not exist.'"

"The teacher must derive not only the capacity, but the desire, to observe natural phenomena. The teacher must understand and feel her position of observer: the activity must lie in the phenomenon."

"We teachers can only help the work going on, as servants wait upon a master."

"It is not enough for the teacher to love the child. She must first love and understand the universe. She must prepare herself, and truly work at it."

"To aid life, leaving it free, however, that is the basic task of the educator."

"We especially need imagination in science. It is not all mathematics, nor all logic, but it is somewhat beauty and poetry."

"No social problem is as universal as the oppression of the child."

"Respect all the reasonable forms of activity in which the child engages and try to understand them."

"Never help a child with a task at which he feels he can succeed."

"We must support as much as possible the child's desires for activity; not wait on him, but educate him to be independent."

FURTHER READING

Maria Montessori: A Biography by Rita Kramer
Maria Montessori: Her Life and Work by E. M. Standing
The Light Within: The Story of Maria Montessori by Norah Smaridge

THE YOUNG MAN AND THE SEA

ADAPTED FROM *THE PEARL KING* BY ROBERT EUNSON

"Your father may be sick for a long time. He might even die. You must find a great strength, for you are the man of the family now."[1]

Being the firstborn of ten children, young Kokichi took his mother's words to heart and immediately assumed his duties as the noodlemaker's son. After helping his mother make the noodles, Kokichi would push the noodle cart with a coal-burning stove out into the streets at night and begin sounding his whistle. Many nights, he didn't get home until two o'clock in the morning, after all of the noodles were sold.

Still, he felt the need to do more. One day, Kokichi saw farmers selling vegetables early in the morning at the market. He decided to do the same, knowing that he would get only two hours of sleep each night. He was only eleven years old. For most of Kokichi's childhood and teenage years, he was trudging the streets, selling vegetables by day and noodles by night. There was little time for play. So, when a friend invited him to go on a trip to Tokyo, he begged his father to let him go. By then, the twenty-year-old had earned a vacation for all his hard work and sacrifice. His dad agreed and gave him more money than he asked for.

For the young villager, the experience of being away from home for the first time opened his eyes and sparked his imagination. While sight-seeing in the big city one day, he saw a group of merchants buying up all the supply of little pearls. When Kokichi asked what the buying spree was about, he was told that the pearls were used for medicinal purposes. This ignited an idea in the young noodlemaker. Maybe he should go into the pearl business, he thought. But this would not happen for a few more years, until after marriage.

Kokichi was twenty-three when he married his seventeen-year-old bride Ume. She turned out to be just the type of woman he needed—

someone who was hardworking and supportive of her husband. But by the time he got into the pearl business, the great demand for pearls nearly made the oysters extinct in Japan.

Kokichi came up with an idea. He suggested farming pearls as a way to meet the growing demand. One village decided to go along with his experiment. On September 11, 1888, the villagers began gathering their first oysters and submerging them at Jinmyo Mura Bay. Meanwhile, he would discuss his dreams with his wife at night.

"How do pearls get there?" he asked.

"Accident," Ume replied.

"If it's an accident, then how can we make it happen on purpose?"[2] Kokichi inquired.

The answer was found by consulting with a marine biologist, Dr. Mizukuri. "What it is that makes pearls in the first place?"[3] Kokichi asked the scientist. What he learned was that a pearl usually begins when a grain of sand or some foreign object enters the oyster by accident. The oyster tries to dispel the irritating particle. When it cannot, the oyster secretes a solution to coat the particle to reduce the irritation. After several years and countless coatings, the pearl is formed.

Excited by what he had learned, he approached his wife with his new plan of growing pearls inside oysters. "If it is what you want," Ume said, "then do it. I will work hard by your side and know in my heart you will be a success."[4]

When none of the first oysters showed any signs of pearls, Kokichi ordered five thousand more by borrowing money. "We must not quit after one failure,"[5] Kokichi declared. "This year we will put out five thousand oysters and try everything we can think of as a kernel to start the pearl."[6]

He and the villagers began experimenting with almost every foreign object to insert inside the oyster's shell, from tiny pieces of shell to bits of broken glass. Some time passed, yet there was still no sign of pearls. The villagers who gave up fishing for farming pearls began to voice their doubts. "Why don't you forget all this silly business about making oysters grow pearls and go back to your noodle shop,"[7] one fisherman said. "Because it is my life's work. I am dedicated to it,"[8] Kokichi asserted.

His wife was quick to provide support. "Let them say anything they want. As long as we love and understand each other, that is all that matters," Ume persuaded. "Now tell me what new idea you have dreamed up this afternoon."[9]

Kokichi had been thinking of a new idea. Why not use bits of mother-of-pearl, the inside layer of the oyster shell, as the seed? Ume agreed. The next morning, husband and wife carried the new oysters seeded with tiny bits of mother-of-pearl to Nishiki-ura Bay. Just as they returned home, they received catastrophic news. The Red Tide, an epidemic of killer plankton, had invaded the waters at Jinmyo Mura Bay, killing all of the oysters and destroying four years of work in the process.

Kokichi was devastated. Nothing Ume said could lift his spirits. Even worse, he couldn't start over because he was broke. When creditors came looking for him, he hid inside the house to avoid them. It was the lowest point in Kokichi's life.

Ume never let her husband forget about his dream. One day in July 1893, Ume dragged her husband to check on the oysters they had planted together at Nishiki-ura Bay. As Ume opened one of the oysters with a knife, the sheen from the white pearl caught her eyes. She immediately called out to her husband. Kokichi ran to his wife and saw her holding an oyster with a pearl inside. "We've done it!"[10] he shouted. They had successfully cultivated the first pearl!

In spite of the success, Kokichi was dissatisfied. The shape of the pearl was semi-circular, not round. Because perfectly round pearls are the rarest of all pearls in nature, they are considered the most beautiful and thus the most lucrative. Nonetheless, news of Kokichi's triumph quickly spread throughout the country. Wasting no time, Kokichi ordered a large-scale production of semi-circular pearls to pay off the debts. Even though the perfect pearl still eluded him, Kokichi was beginning to regain his confidence.

Then suddenly, tragedy struck. Ume, at age thirty-two, died from complications after having surgery to remove one of her ovaries that was infected. In her last moment, Ume's loving words soothed her husband's grief by urging him to go on with his work. And so he did. By January 1905, he had one million oysters in the sea. Thousands of them were being experimented with new seeding methods and different materials. Yet, the perfect pearl was nowhere to be found.

Then, on January 10, 1905, the terrible Red Tide came back. Of the one million oysters, eight hundred fifty thousand died. This was a great catastrophe, but Kokichi refused to accept defeat, even from nature. Day after day, he kept busy by opening thousands of dead oysters, hoping to find a perfectly round pearl. One day, he opened an oyster. Seeing no pearl, he probed into the soft belly and there he found the perfect pearl. Excited, Kokichi opened four more oysters from the same basket. The results were the same. All of these oysters were inseminated with mother-of-pearl that was completely buried in living tissue. At last, after fifteen years, he had achieved his ultimate dream. He got nature to cooperate!

By the end of his life, Kokichi's oysters were producing ten million world-famous pearls annually. Who was this Pearl King?

KOKICHI MIKIMOTO

When one pursues one's dream and never gives up in spite of life's most difficult challenges, eventually the dream becomes reality. For Kokichi Mikimoto, he won over many adversities, even against nature.

KOKICHI MIKIMOTO'S BIO

Birth Name: Kokichi Mikimoto
Birthplace: Toba, Japan
Birth Date: March 10, 1858
Died: September 21, 1954
Age: Ninety-six years old

ACHIEVEMENTS AND AWARDS

1893:   Cultured the world's first semi-round pearls

1905:   Cultured the world's first round pearls

1913:   Opening of overseas stores

1927:   Paid visit to Thomas Edison

During their meeting, Edison said, "It is one of the wonders of the world that you were able to culture pearls." Mikimoto replied modestly, "If you were the moon of the world of inventors, I am nothing more than one of its countless stars." Edison was so touched by this remark that he covered his eyes and wept.

1930:   The Japanese government nominated Mikimoto as one of the top ten inventors in the country

Richard Lam

Selected Quotes by Kokichi Mikimoto

"We must not quit after one failure."

"If it's an accident, then how can we make it happen on purpose?"

"A man with a home, a good wife, and a job is the only truly happy one—therefore a rich one."

"I would like to adorn the necks of all the women of the world with pearls."

Further Reading

The Pearl King: The Story of the Fabulous Mikimoto by Robert Eunson

SHOOTING STAR

Poor Phoebe. Her father died of pneumonia when she was five. The loss of the breadwinner left the huge burden of raising the four younger children in the family to Mom and Phoebe's oldest sister, Mary Jane. Then, a little more than a year later, tragedy struck again. Mary Jane contracted tuberculosis and died. Almost everything was sold to pay for the doctor's bills and funeral expenses. Not much was left for food.

It was at this time that seven-year-old Phoebe began using her clever mind. She learned to trap quails by making contraptions to capture the birds, which served as a source of meat the family desperately needed. Still, she wanted to do more. One day while her mother was at work, Phoebe climbed on a bench to get her father's rifle that hung over the mantelpiece. As she loaded the gun with gunpowder, she unknowingly spilled some in front of the fireplace. When her mother asked who had been playing with the rifle, Phoebe admitted it, then immediately persuaded her mother to let her shoot rabbits. Not long after, Phoebe was providing enough wild game meat for the whole family.

The family's standard of living improved and even more so when Mom remarried an old widower who had some money. Sadly, a year and half later, Phoebe's stepfather died, leaving behind a new member of the family, a baby sister. Tough times returned. To lessen the financial burden, Mom decided it was best that Phoebe stay with a friend, Mrs. Eddington, who worked at a shelter for the poor. In exchange for her help, Phoebe was given room and board and schooling.

Less than a year later, when Phoebe heard that a farmer wanted to hire a young girl to take care of his baby, she jumped at the chance to make money even though she would be forty miles away from home. Little did she know what lay ahead with the Wolf family.

At the Wolf farm, this poor eight-year-old girl was forced to work like a slave from dawn to dusk cooking, cleaning, feeding the farm animals, and taking care of the baby. When she fell asleep due to exhaustion, the Wolf lady would yell and hit her. Communication between Phoebe and her mother was cut off. Phoebe never saw the letters Mom sent. As if this wasn't cruel enough, the Wolf lady fabricated letters in her mother's name encouraging her to work hard and be a good girl. Then she sent letters home lying to Mom that Phoebe was enjoying her stay and going to school.

Time after time, the child begged to go home. "If you ask that again, I'll cut your liver and heart out and hang them on a fence stake for the crows to pick,"[1] the Wolf lady threatened. Day after day, she toiled and suffered, for two years. All this while, she thought her fifty cents per week earning, as promised, were being sent home to support her family. Mom never received a penny. Finally, one day, Phoebe summoned the courage to run away. When she got home and told Mom about her unforgettable experience, Mom was furious.

Phoebe never forgot that torturous experience, but she didn't dwell on it for long. She quickly returned to what she did best to help out the family. Her hunting, trapping, and shooting were so good that she ended up with surpluses of wild game, which was sold to a hotel keeper for a profit. Soon, this fifteen-year-old was able to pay off the entire two-hundred-dollar mortgage on the family farm with the money she earned. "Oh, how my heart leaped with joy as I handed the money to mother and told her that I had saved enough to pay it off!"[2] Phoebe rejoiced.

During this time, in the 1870s, from age ten to fifteen, Phoebe began trick-shooting for many hours in the woods, often against her mother's will. As she honed her skills, she dreamt of being a champion shot, perhaps the best shooter in her state of Ohio. She didn't know it yet, but her skills with the rifle would reward her more than she could ever imagine.

One day, Phoebe was invited to visit her older sister, Lyda, and Lyda's husband, Joseph Stein, in Cincinnati. Joseph was well aware of the wild game his sister-in-law was sending to his friend and hotel owner, Mr. Frost. The two men belonged to the same gun club.

After watching a shooting contest one day, Joseph turned to Mr. Frost and boasted, "That's nothing. I have a kid sister-in-law at my house that can beat the socks off that fellow."[3]

"Bring her out and we will have a match between them Thanksgiving Day,"[4] Mr. Frost suggested.

Mr. Frost was so interested in this match that he put up fifty dollars as the prize. For Joseph, there was good reason to be so confident in his sister-in-law's skills. Each one of Phoebe's wild animals was shot through the head!

Come the day of the match, the touring champion, Frank Butler, asked who the little girl carrying a gun was. When he learned that Phoebe was to be his opponent, Frank thought it was a prank and laughed. The final score was twenty-five to twenty-four in favor of Phoebe. She shot down all twenty-five clay pigeons and took home the prize. Frank was impressed, in more ways than one. Phoebe's shooting skills were one thing, but it was her grace and charm that won Frank's heart that day. Nine months later, they were married. Together, they would embark on a long and successful career doing road shows in America and abroad.

After a few years of performing trick shooting stunts with the Sells Brothers Circus, the highly entertaining couple was hired by Buffalo Bill Cody to perform in his popular Wild West Show in March 1885. Over the next seventeen years, the act performed by Phoebe and Frank was always a crowd favorite. Phoebe always had the spotlight because of her amazing skills while Frank served as her assistant and stunt choreographer.

The stunts mesmerized spectators everywhere. Phoebe would stand on a horse's back and break the glass balls by shooting them as Frank threw the balls in the air while riding alongside her. As Frank held a playing card between his fingers with the card edge facing Phoebe, she would cut the card in half with a single bullet using a pistol from ninety feet away. When Frank tossed six glass balls in the air, she shot them all before any hit the ground.

Frank always added new tricks to keep the act fresh and entertaining. This meant that Phoebe had to practice constantly to learn new tricks and to sharpen her skills so that she could perform flawlessly. Over the years, millions of fans from the United States and Europe showered her with applause and cheers. Some of Europe's royalty presented gifts, honors, and medals to her.

She always accepted the challenge of a shooting match and won against nearly all of the world's best shooters, who were predominately men. As her fame and fortunes grew, she never forgot her roots or that horrific childhood experience. She always sent money home to Mom and visited her family during her time off. Lots of poor children were able to see the show for free because Phoebe often raised the tent behind the seats to let them in.

She became the most famous woman in her time. Who was this
shooting star with such a generous heart?

ANNIE OAKLEY

Phoebe Ann Moses changed her name to Annie Oakley. Oftentimes it is our adversities that determine our character and genius.

ANNIE OAKLEY'S BIO

Birth Name:	Phoebe Ann Moses
Birthplace:	near Willowdell, Ohio, United States
Birth Date:	August 13, 1860
Died:	November 3, 1926
Age:	Sixty-six years old

AMAZING STUNTS

On various occasions, Annie hit 483 out of 500, 943 out of 1,000, and 4,772 out of 5,000 targets.

She defeated nearly all of the world-class shooters who challenged her.

With a single shot from a distance, she extinguished the cigarette held in the mouth of Crown Prince Wilhem of Germany.

She broke clay pigeons thrown from traps not only one at a time, but as many as four at a time.

Frank would swing a cord around his body, at the end of which was a glass ball; Annie would lie backward over a chair, and with her gun upside down, would break the ball.

Annie held a pistol backward over her shoulder and using a silver knife for a mirror, would break a ball tied to the end of a string, which Frank whirled around his body.

Annie would ride around on a bicycle without holding on to the handlebars and shoot objects thrown into the air.

Richard Lam

SELECTED QUOTES BY ANNIE OAKLEY

"I always preferred taking my shot when the game was on the move. It gave them a fair chance and made me quick of eye and hand."

"I believe that God gives everybody a talent, and if she develops it and makes money it is not right to squander that money in selfish, extravagant living, but she must try to do good with it."

"I've made a good deal of money in my time, but I never believe in wasting a dollar of it."

"I believe in simple living."

"I've been near death four times in my life and the Good Lord had always pulled me through. He'll pull me through this time too. I'll shoot again, and I'll be as good as ever."

FURTHER READING

Missie by Anne Fern Swartwout
Annie Oakley by Shirl Kasper
The Life and Legacy of Annie Oakley by Glenda Riley

PEACE BY PEACE

No one could have ever imagined what Karamchand was able to achieve, not even himself.

"I was a coward. I used to be haunted by the fear of thieves, ghosts, and serpents. Darkness was a terror to me. I could not bear to sleep without a light in the room,"[1] he said. In primary school, he was a mediocre student who was very shy. "As soon as school closed, I literally ran back because I could not bear to talk to anybody. I was even afraid lest anyone should poke fun at me,"[2] Karamchand said.

But whatever fears he had, he certainly wasn't afraid to follow his conscience and do the right thing at a young age. At fifteen, he stole a bit of gold from his brother's armlet to pay off his brother's debt. Even though his intention was good, Karamchand couldn't bear the guilt of stealing. So he wrote his father a note asking for forgiveness. "In this note not only did I confess my guilt, but I asked adequate punishment for it, and closed with a request to him not to punish himself for my offense. I also pledged myself never to steal in the future,"[3] he said.

As Dad read the note, tears trickled down his cheeks and dripped on the paper. He closed his eyes for a moment and then tore up the note. "Those pearl-drops of love cleansed my heart, and washed my sin away. I know that my confession made my father feel absolutely safe about me, and increased his affection for me beyond measure,"[4] Karamchand recalled. That was the end of his sins.

Academically, Karamchand had always been a mediocre student, all the way through high school. Somehow, he passed his college entrance examinations in 1887. Even though academics were never Karamchand's strong suit, his family still insisted that he go to college. But college proved too difficult. At the end of the first term, he returned home not knowing what to do next. An old friend and advisor of the family suggested that he go to England to study law. It would be easier to become a lawyer there. His brother agreed and promised to provide the financial support. However, his mother was reluctant to let him go for fear that he would pick up bad habits overseas.

To alleviate his mother's fears, he promised not to touch wine, women, and meat. Mom finally approved. So in 1888, at age eighteen, Karamchand sailed for England, leaving his wife and newborn son behind. He was only thirteen when he married his wife, Kasturba, in an arranged marriage. After three years of law school, he came home with his diploma in hand and his vow unbroken. But there would be no celebration. Upon his return, he was struck with tremendous grief on learning of his mother's death. His brother had kept the terrible news from him so that he could concentrate on his studies. "My grief was even greater than over my father's death,"[5] he said. But he got over his terrible loss rather quickly.

There were pressing matters at hand. He had to find a job to support his family and repay his brother. With his brother's help, he landed a low-paying legal position where he took on his first case in a small claims court. On cross-examining the plaintiff's witnesses, he got so nervous that he became speechless. "I hastened from the court, not knowing whether my client won or lost her case, but I was ashamed of myself and decided not to take up any more cases until I had courage enough to conduct them,"[6] he confessed. However, it didn't take long to change his mind when a job opened up in Natal, South Africa.

The temptations of seeing a new country, gaining new experience, and receiving a high salary were just too good to resist.

So, in 1898, he set sail again, leaving his wife and now two sons behind for a one-year contract. This decision would change his life forever. Upon arrival in South Africa, Karamchand learned quickly that life was going to be a struggle. Because of his dark skin, he was forced to leave the first-class compartment of the train even though he had a first-class ticket. When he refused, he was kicked off the train and left shivering in the winter cold inside the train station.

As he sat there, he began questioning his duty. "Should I fight for my rights or go back home, or should I go on without minding the insults, and return home after finishing the case?"[7] he pondered. He thought that to go home would be cowardice. "I should try, if possible to root out the disease and suffer hardships in the process,"[8] he decided. Karamchand had found his courage.

But first he had to help settle a lawsuit over a large sum of money. He studied every detail about the case. By working alongside the best attorneys in town, Karamchand sharpened his skills and gained more confidence. When Karamchand suggested a compromise between the two parties where the defendant was allowed to make repayments in installments, the case was settled. "I had learnt to find out the better side of human nature and to enter men's hearts,"[9] he rejoiced. He had fought for his client and won.

Having fulfilled his contract, instead of going home, he extended his stay. He had promised himself to fight against the white government of South Africa. During his one-year stay, he witnessed many acts of discrimination and exploitation against his people, all because of their skin color. His one-year contract became a twenty-year tour of duty in which he fought for equal rights for his countrymen who were living in a foreign land. Not once did he resort to violence against his opponents. Instead, he wrote and spoke out publicly against the oppression of his people. In 1894, he founded the Natal Indian Congress, an organization established to unite his people against the British government in South Africa. Soon, the Indian community rallied around him as their leader. With his people now behind him, Karamchand organized and led peaceful demonstrations and marches, urging his people not to retaliate against attacks, no matter how violent things got.

In the beginning of this nonviolent civil rights movement, the South African government tried very hard to crush the spirit of the Indian people. Thousands of men, women, and children were jailed, including Karamchand. Some were flogged or even shot for civil disobedience. In spite of all the attacks, Karamchand continued to fight on using his method of warfare: mass nonviolent protest. He believed this was the only way to fight and win. His people believed it, too. Soon, more and more peaceful demonstrations spread across South Africa. Karamchand's mass nonviolent resistance method worked. Over time, the South African government gave in and repealed the most abusive laws against Karamchand's people. But his fight wasn't finished yet.

The people who ruled South Africa also ruled Karamchand's country. In 1915, he returned home for the fight of his life. Following his success in South Africa, he inspired his country to adopt his new method of warfare on a much larger scale. Karamchand urged his people to boycott British goods, educational institutions, and government services and to resign from government employment. When the British imposed a tax on salt, Karamchand protested by leading his people on a 248-mile march to the sea in March 1930. The government responded by putting thousands of protesters in jail. In the summer of 1934, three unsuccessful attempts were made on his life, yet he continued to lead his people in the fight for independence.

The British arrested Karamchand and his followers in the capital city of Bombay in August 1942 and put him under house arrest for two years in the Aga Khan Palace in Pune. It was here that he suffered another terrible blow. His wife died after serving eighteen months in prison in February 1944. Nothing could stop him now. He was willing to fight to the end. Finally, after more than 200 years of British rule, India, under Karamchand's leadership, regained its independence on August 15, 1947.

This soft-spoken lawyer led his people to overthrow an empire. Who was this nonviolent revolutionary?

MOHANDAS GANDHI

Mohandas Gandhi proved that the best way to win over hatred, prejudice, and injustice is through nonviolent means. His life inspired many great leaders.

MOHANDAS GANDHI'S BIO

Birth Name: Mohandas Karamchand Gandhi
Birthplace: Porbander, India
Birth Date: October, 2 1869
Died: January, 30 1948
Age: Seventy-eight years old

ACHIEVEMENTS AND AWARDS

Fought for equal rights for Indians in South Africa

Founded the Natal Indian Congress in South Africa in 1894

Led the famous 248-mile Salt March in India from Sabarmati Ashram to Dandi, Gujarat from March 12 to April 6 in 1930

Freed India from British rule

In India, he is honored as the *Father of the Nation*. His birthday, October 2, is recognized as a national holiday in India and as the International Day of Nonviolence throughout the world.

Selected Quotes by Mohandas Gandhi

"We must be the change we wish to see."

"The best way to find yourself is to lose yourself in the service of others."

"An eye for an eye makes the whole world blind."

"There are many causes that I am prepared to die for but no causes that I am prepared to kill for."

"The first thing you have to learn about history is that because something has not taken place in the past, that does not mean it cannot take place in the future."

"A clean confession, combined with a promise never to commit the sin again, when offered before one who has the right to receive it, is the purest type of repentance."

"Infinite striving for perfection is one's right. It is its own reward."

"Sacrifice is the law of life. We can do nothing or get nothing without paying a price for it."

"All of your scholarship, all of your study of Shakespeare and Wordsworth would be vain if at the same time you did not build your character and attain mastery of your thoughts and your actions."

"Purity of life is the highest and truest art."

"Does not the history of the world show that there would have been no romance in life if there had been no risks?"

"The law of love could be best understood and learned through little children."

"My notion of democracy is that under it the weakest should have the same opportunity as the strongest."

"A nation that is capable of limitless sacrifice is capable of rising to limitless heights. The purer the sacrifice the quicker the progress."

"Good travels at a snail's pace. Those who want to do good are not selfish, they are not in a hurry, they know that to impregnate people with good requires a long time."

"Nonviolence should never be used as a shield for the cowardice. It is a weapon for the brave."

"The force generated by nonviolence is infinitely greater than the force of all the arms invented by man's ingenuity."

"You cannot shake hands with a clenched fist."

"The weak can never forgive. Forgiveness is the attribute of the strong."

"You must not lose faith in humanity. Humanity is an ocean; if a few drops of the ocean are dirty, the ocean does not become dirty."

"Always aim at complete harmony of thought and word and deed. Always aim at purifying your thoughts and everything will be well."

"Happiness is when what you think, what you say, and what you do are in harmony."

"Freedom is not worth having if it does not include the freedom to make mistakes."

"There is more to life than increasing its speed."

"When I despair, I remember that all through history the ways of truth and love have always won. There have been tyrants, and murderers, and

Richard Lam

for a time they can seem invincible, but in the end they always fall. Think of it—always."

"Honest differences are often a healthy sign of progress."

"Where there is love there is life."

FURTHER READING

The Essential Writings of Mahatma Gandhi by Mahatma Gandhi
Gandhi, the Man: The Story of His Transformation by Eknath Easwaran
Autobiography: The Story of My Experiments with Truth by Mohandas K. Gandhi

Iron Will

One day, Bessie overheard a man calling her father a fool for educating his girls. "My daughters have as good minds as my sons. I see no reason why they should not be taught to use them. As to what use they will put them to in later life, that will be for them to decide,"[1] Papa rebuked. Aside from being nonconforming, Papa was also very stubborn and ambitious. Young Bessie would inherit her father's traits.

The family sugar business was failing in Bristol, England, so Papa decided to uproot the family and move to America to start all over. Bessie arrived in New York City with her family in August 1832. Soon after, Bessie was back in school and began to enjoy living in her new environment. Later, the family moved to Cincinnati, Ohio, with the prospect of opening a sugar refinery there. Within three months, the extreme heat during the summer of 1828 proved too much for Papa. After a short illness, he died from bilious fever, the result of a liver dysfunction. Papa's sudden departure left his wife and nine children to fend for themselves.

At age seventeen, Bessie immediately assumed the role as the head of the household. She proposed opening a boarding school in her home for much-needed income. In time, Bessie and her two older sisters, Anna and Marian, were teaching young girls at their in-home day and boarding school. While the money from the tuition helped support the family, Bessie soon realized that teaching young children didn't quite suit her. Yet, her restless mind couldn't quite settle on the few career choices that were available to women at the time.

One day, Bessie paid a visit to a close friend, Mary Donaldson, who was dying of cancer. As she was about to leave, Mary stopped her. "Wait dear. For some time I've wanted to say something to you,"[2] Mary intimated. "It's a terrible thing to die a slow death like this, but there's one thing that would have made the suffering so much easier for me.

If … if only I didn't have to be examined and treated by a man!" she regretted. "You are fond of study, have health and leisure; why not study medicine?"[3] Mary recommended. Bessie said she would consider it.

She did not make any promises. After all, she found the subject of physiology to be rather distasteful. "I hated everything connected with the body, and could not bear the sight of a medical book,"[4] she said. But the words of her dying friend lingered.

Before she made up her mind, Bessie bravely posed the question to her family. Being independent thinkers, her family applauded her idea of being a doctor. Having the family support was a good start, but she had no idea where to begin. So she asked family friends and wrote to physicians for advice. The responses were unanimous. No way! They pointed out that while the idea was a good one, it was impossible to accomplish. A number of reasons were given. First, no medical school admitted women. Second, the education was long and expensive. Last, too many obstacles had to be overcome.

Instead of being discouraged, Bessie took the disappointing news as motivation. "If an idea was really a valuable one," she reasoned, "there must be some way of realizing it."[5] The more she thought about the idea of winning a medical degree the more she believed in achieving her goal. At the same time, she was beginning to see this not only as a personal challenge but also a challenge to change society's perception of woman as doctors. "The moral fight possessed immense attraction for me,"[6] she said.

So, in the summer of 1847, she moved in with family friends in Philadelphia, the center of medical learning at the time. She applied to the top medical schools in Philadelphia and New York City. She had no luck. After applying to twenty-nine medical schools, one finally accepted her: Geneva Medical School in western New York State. This was not supposed to happen, however. Her acceptance was a strange twist of fate. Normally, the faculty selected the applicants for admission. But this time, the faculty delegated the job to the all-male student body to vote on Bessie's application. The faculty had assumed that the student body would quickly reject the female applicant just as they would have. But things didn't turn out that way. Some students held outright prejudice against her. Some were rather curious. And some realized the historic significance of this vote. In the end, after some debate, Bessie was accepted.

At Geneva, she quickly won the respect of her classmates and faculty with her work ethic and intelligence. Two years later, she became the first woman to graduate from an American medical school, beating out all her classmates to win top honors. But her diploma was useless. No hospital or clinic would hire her. Even women didn't trust their own kind as doctors. Frustrated by endless rejections, she left for Paris, France. There, a physician who was a family friend suggested to Bessie that she would benefit by getting training at La Maternite, where peasant women were trained as midwives.

At La Maternite, Bessie endured poor working conditions. The air was bad and so was the food. On the average, she lost sleep every fifth night while delivering babies. Yet, her experience at La Maternite was invaluable as she gained a great deal of knowledge and confidence in the field of obstetrics. Then disaster struck. One early morning, Bessie was treating a baby with a severe case of ophthalmia, an inflammation of the eye that is highly contagious and can result in blindness. As she sprayed the baby's eye, some of the water splattered onto her left eye. It became inflamed overnight. Horrified, Bessie realized she had contracted the dreadful disease.

After exhausting all remedies, the left eye could not be saved. Later, her left eye had to be removed and replaced with an artificial one that was made out of glass. Her dreams of becoming a surgeon were shattered. While Bessie was recovering from her trauma, a letter from St. Bartholomew's Hospital, one of the best in London, England, granted her admission as a student. The news was bittersweet because she could no longer do surgery with just one eye. Nonetheless, she went to London and gained some more valuable experience. She would have stayed in England, but with no job and no money and being away from her family, she had to return to America.

Back home, her bad luck continued. Bessie established a private practice in New York City, but very few patients came. She applied as a physician at a large, city dispensary. Again, she was turned down even with all her credentials. But she didn't give up.

After seeing so many poor people in desperate need of health care, she just had to do something about it. So, with the financial help from her friends, she opened her own dispensary in one of the worst slums in the city in 1853, offering her services for free. In this single rented room, women who were too sick to worry about seeing a woman doctor came for treatment. Bessie was soon overwhelmed with patients. She made house calls at all hours of the day and night. In addition to treating sicknesses and delivering babies, Bessie lectured mothers about prevention, hygiene, and cleanliness. These ideas were so revolutionary at the time that it took the medical profession fifty years to catch up.

Later, Bessie opened a hospital for women and children and a medical college for women. The coursework at her college was more rigorous than all the rest. Who was this first woman doctor in America and medical pioneer?

ELIZABETH BLACKWELL

Through determination, perseverance, and sacrifice, Elizabeth Blackwell proved to the world that a female doctor is as equally good as a male doctor. She forced open the doors of the medical profession for all women.

ELIZABETH BLACKWELL'S BIO

Birth Name: Elizabeth Blackwell
Birthplace: Bristol, England
Birth Date: February 3, 1821
Died: May 31, 1910
Age: Eighty-nine years old

ACHIEVEMENTS

Opened the New York Infirmary for Women and Children in 1857

Opened the Women's Medical College of the New York Infirmary in 1868

New York Infirmary became the first training school for nurses in America

Helped establish the London School of Medicine for Women in 1875 and became the leading professor of hygiene

Helped establish the London's New Hospital for Women

Helped establish the National Health Society

Selected Quotes by Elizabeth Blackwell

"I have to become a surgeon. It's my—my divine calling. And nothing, nobody on earth is going to stop me."

"If an idea is valuable, there must be a way of realizing it."

"It is not easy to be a pioneer—but oh, it is fascinating! I would not trade one moment, even the worst moment, for all the riches in the world."

"With common sense, self-reliance, and attention to the work at hand, any woman can pursue the medical calling without risk."

"What special contribution can women make to medicine? Not blind imitation of men, nor thoughtless acceptance of whatever may be taught by them, for this would endorse the widespread error that the human race consists chiefly of men. Our duty is loyalty to the right and opposition to the wrong, in accordance with the essential principles of our own nature."

"It is better to prevent disease than to cure it."

"Nature, with its God-given remedies of fresh air, cleanliness, exercise, is the world's best doctor."

"If society will not admit of woman's free development, then society must be remodeled."

"Our school education ignores, in a thousand ways, the rules of healthy development."

Further Reading

Pioneer Work in Opening the Medical Profession to Women by Elizabeth Blackwell

Lone Woman by Dorothy Clarke Wilson

I Will Be Doctor, The Story of America's First Woman Physician by Dorothy Clarke Wilson

The First Woman Doctor: The Story of Elizabeth Blackwell by Corinne Malvern

DREAMS DO COME TRUE

"Once you've lived through the worst, you're never quite as vulnerable afterwards,"[1] Elias once said. And he was right.

For Elias, his worst experience began at the tender age of ten. Every morning, he and his older brother Roy had to wake up at 3:30 to deliver newspapers for two hours. To make matters more challenging, their dad's strict order for quality work demanded that newspapers be placed behind screen doors, not tossed on doorsteps. "I remember those icy cold days of crawling up these icy steps. I was so darn cold, I'd slip and I could cry, so I cried,"[2] Elias remembered.

By the time he got to school, Elias was too exhausted to concentrate on his lessons. Then right after school, he had to hurry back to the newspaper office to get the afternoon edition and make the rounds a second time. So, it was no surprise that his grades were poor. But Elias did surprise everyone with his talent for drawing. Dad gladly paid for art classes at the Kansas City Art Institute. In addition to drawing, Elias developed an interest in performing. He teamed up with a classmate and performed every chance they got, often imitating Charlie Chaplin.

When Elias graduated from grammar school in 1917, he dreamt of combining his talents of drawing and comedy into cartoons, a new art form at the time. But his plans had to wait. Dad had decided to invest a large sum of money in a jelly factory in Chicago. So Elias and his family moved back to his birthplace where he enrolled in Chicago's McKinley High School. There, he pursued his passion and drew cartoons for the school newspaper.

In the evenings, he headed to the Chicago Academy of Fine Arts three times a week for more advanced instruction on drawing cartoons. He often attended vaudeville shows and took notes of the best jokes, new ideas, and things that didn't work. He took on a number of part-time jobs to pay for his art classes and entertainment expenses. After a year of high school, he decided to drop out to join his brother in the First World War. But he was too young for military service. So he volunteered as an ambulance driver for the Red Cross instead.

By the time the Red Cross sent Elias over to France, the war was over and the post-war restoration began. When he wasn't busy, he honed his drawing skills by drawing posters for the Red Cross and sketches for his friends. He had decided to become a newspaper cartoonist when he returned home. But Dad already had a different plan for him—a job at the jelly factory. Elias rejected the offer and insisted on pursuing his dream.

After an exchange of harsh words between father and son, Elias left home for good and headed back to Kansas City, reuniting with Roy. With his portfolio in hand, he immediately set out to find a job as a newspaper cartoonist. No luck. Both major newspapers rejected him. At Roy's suggestion, Elias accepted a temporary position at a commercial art studio. There, he drew farm animals for a farm equipment catalog.

Within a few weeks, both Elias and his new friend, Ub Iwerks, were laid off due to lack of business. Soon after, these two young artists decided to team up and open their own studio. However, their new venture failed after only a month. Several weeks later, Elias landed a job at the Kansas City Film Ad Company. Ub soon came aboard thanks to a good recommendation from Elias.

The ad company produced primitive one-minute advertising films that were shown before the feature presentation at movie houses. Elias found the animation outdated. So, he went to the Kansas City Public Library and read everything he could find about cartoons and animation. Then, he borrowed a camera from his boss and used a garage as a studio to experiment with his own animated films.

After working many late nights, Elias produced several cartoons and approached his boss with the idea of making cartoons for the company. But his boss turned him down. So, he went out on his own. In May 1922, with fifteen thousand dollars from a number of local investors, he established Laugh-O-Gram Films, Inc. Ub and several other young artists from the former employer joined the new company.

Two seven-minute films were produced: *Puss in Boots* and *Red Riding Hood*. These two films did well enough in local theaters to convince Elias to hire salesmen to sell the films to movie houses nationwide. But none of the salesmen turned over any money. A year later, the company was in deep financial trouble. "It was probably the blackest time of my life,"[3] Elias said later. "I really knew what hardship and hunger were like."[4] He was now living out of his small downtown office and eating beans out of a can and leftover bread. For a dime, he allowed himself the luxury of a bath at the Union Station once a week. Despite these hardships, he wasn't going to give up. He wanted to give one last try at success.

With the help of Ub and a few student animators, Elias poured all of his energy and what money was left into another film called *Alice's Wonderland*. But before the film could be completed, the company ran out of money and filed for bankruptcy. When Roy heard the news, he wrote his younger brother from Los Angeles, "Call it quits, kid. You can't do anything more than you've already done."[5] He asked Elias to go west and join him. In yet another bold move, Elias left for Hollywood with only fifty dollars in his pocket and the unfinished film in his suitcase.

He stayed with his Uncle Robert and began looking for work at all the major movie studios. He wanted to be a director but had no such luck. No movie studio wanted to hire him. Demoralized and destitute, he had no choice but to return to what he was doing before. So he finished *Alice's Wonderland* and sold it to Margaret Winkler, a New York film distributor, who liked it so much that she immediately ordered six new films based on the same character. Elias was back in business.

In 1923, the two brothers formed a new studio. Roy took care of the company's finances while Elias directed the films. After making twenty films based on the *Alice* series, Ub was brought on board to help improve the films. By then, the *Alice* series was getting old. So Margaret suggested a new character, *Oswald the Lucky Rabbit*.

The new *Oswald* films quickly became popular. Business was going well for Elias and company. Then, in spring 1928, disaster struck. Elias and his wife Lilly decided to take a trip out to New York to renew his contract for more *Oswald* films. When Elias asked the new film distributor Charlie Mintz for more money, he was betrayed. Mintz had lured away all of his staff except for Ub. And because Mintz owned the copyrights to the cartoons, Elias was forced to make one of two choices—either work for Mintz or lose everything.

Elias was disgusted. "I renounce my rights to *Oswald the Lucky Rabbit*! I don't want him anymore! Just trying to draw him after all this would make me sick to my stomach!"[6] he fumed at Mintz. On his train ride back to California, he started thinking of a new cartoon character. After some doodling and a few sketches, he pitched the idea to his wife. "What do you think of the name Mortimer Mouse?"[7] Elias asked. "Mortimer? That's a funny name for a mouse," Lilly countered. "How about Mickey?"[8]

From that moment on, the world of animation and entertainment was never the same.

Richard Lam

Elias made the world believe in dreams and fairy tales with his animated films. Who was this artistic visionary?

WALT DISNEY

Walt Disney gave the world a new form of entertainment. He showed us that dreams do come true if you are willing to work hard and not give up.

Walt Disney's Bio

Birth Name: Walt Elias Disney
Birthplace: Chicago, Illinois, United States
Birth Date: December 5, 1901
Died: December 15, 1966
Age: Sixty-five years old

Achievements and Awards

Mickey Mouse
Snow White and the Seven Dwarfs
Pinocchio
Fantasia
Bambi
Dumbo
Cinderella
Etc.

Disneyland

Disney World

Walt Disney holds the record for the most Academy Award nominations, with fifty-nine, and the most Oscars, with twenty-six.

Selected Quotes by Walt Disney

"If you can dream it, you can do it."

"I dream, I test my dreams against my beliefs, I dare to take risks, and I execute my vision to make those dreams come true."

"When you're curious, you find lots of interesting things to do. And one thing it takes to accomplish something is courage."

"When you believe a thing, believe it all over, implicitly and unquestionably."

"It's kind of fun to do the impossible."

"The way to get started is to quit talking and begin doing."

"I have been up against tough competition all my life. I wouldn't know how to get along without it."

"You reach a point where you don't work for money."

"Of all of our inventions for mass communication, pictures still speak the most universally understood language."

"Once you've lived through the worst, you're never quite as vulnerable afterwards."

"I only hope that we don't lose sight of one thing—that it was all started by a mouse."

Further Reading

Disney's World by Leonard Mosley
The Magic Kingdom by Steven Watts
Walt Disney: The Triumph of the American Imagination by Neal Gabler

THE PURSUIT OF HAPPINESS

Araminta Ross had an awfully painful childhood. The scars on her head and neck proved it.

One day, she was hired out as a housekeeper and babysitter for a woman named Miss Susan. Right away, Araminta had to face the cruelty of her new employer. Araminta was ordered to dust off the furniture and piano, so she rushed through her task as quickly as possible. What she didn't know was that her haste caused a cloud of dust to form, and soon everything that was cleaned was now covered with dust again. But instead of teaching Araminta, Miss Susan took out the whip and punished her with a number of lashes. Araminta suffered more lashes each time she could not keep the baby sleeping quietly through the night. It wasn't long before the abuse took its toll on little Araminta. Battered and malnourished, she was discharged home for recuperation. She was only five years old.

Mom quickly nursed her child back to health, only to have her return to Miss Susan. More abuse followed. One day, in the middle of a heated argument between Miss Susan and her husband, Araminta decided to steal a lump of sugar. Just as she put her fingers in the sugar bowl, Miss Susan turned around and saw her. She immediately reached for the whip, but Araminta made a mad dash out the door. She ran as far as she could until exhaustion forced her to find shelter inside a large pigpen.

"There I stayed from Friday until the next Tuesday, fighting with those little pigs for potato peelings and other scraps that came down in the trough,"[1] she said. Finally, starvation forced Araminta to face the wrath of Miss Susan once more. "I was so starved I knowed I'd got to go back to my Missus, I hadn't got nowhere else to go, but I knowed what was coming,"[2] she said. This time it was Miss Susan's husband who carried out the punishment. He snuck up from behind and delivered a powerful blow to her side, breaking her ribs.

Once again, Araminta was discharged and returned home, debilitated and starved. And again, Mom nursed her back to health, but the rib injury would pain her for the rest of her life. She never went back to work for that abusive woman. For her remaining childhood years, Araminta continued to do domestic labor for various mistresses or female heads of households. As she got older, she became wiser. If the mistress was abusive, she would put on all the thick clothes she could to protect herself from the whip.

By the time she reached adolescence, Araminta was reassigned to work in the fields, where she learned to hoe and harvest. It was during this time that she suffered her most painful injury. One night, she went to a nearby dry goods store to buy a few things. When she got to the store, a black man was fleeing from his captor. The captor ordered Araminta to stop the fugitive, but she refused. So the captor quickly grabbed a two-pound metal weight from the counter and threw it at the running fugitive. Unfortunately, the weight missed the intended target and struck Araminta in the back of the head, breaking her skull. She was bleeding and fainting as she was carried back to the house, where she was laid to rest on a bench without any medical treatment.

After two days, she went back to the field. "I went to work again and there I worked with the blood and sweat rolling down my face till I couldn't see,"[3] Araminta said. For the third time, she returned home under her mother's care. Araminta never fully recovered from her head injury. For the rest of her life, she experienced uncontrollable episodes of short sleeping spells that caused her to lose concentration and fall into a trance right in the middle of a conversation or while working several times a day.

After her head injury had healed, she went to work for a local entrepreneur named John Stewart sometime around 1835. For the next five years, under Stewart's order, Araminta took on the same responsibilities as the men. At only five feet tall, her strength and ability to drive oxen, plow fields, chop logs, and haul timber impressed not only her boss but the male workers as well. These male workers were black people who were mostly slaves, but some were free of bondage.

Araminta became part of this community of freed and enslaved black people and developed a network of friends. One of her friends was a freed black man named John whom she later married in 1844 at the age of nineteen. After marrying John, Araminta decided to change her first name and adopt her husband's last name. However, marrying a freed man and changing her name did not change the fact that she was still a slave. The only way to be free was to escape to the North. But she didn't know how, and her husband was against it.

By September 1849, Araminta was forced to act. There were rumors that her master was going to sell her at auction. So, she took off on September 17 with her two brothers, Harry and Ben, leaving her husband behind. After several days on the run, they returned because her two brothers feared being captured. If caught, they would either face severe punishment or be sold into the deep South, where they would be forever separated from their family and friends.

Two weeks later, Araminta ran away again, by herself, this time for good. She traveled by night, using the North Star as her compass and instructions from a network of white and black anti-slavery supporters who directed her from one house to the next until she reached Philadelphia. "When I found I had crossed that line," Araminta later recalled, "I looked at my hands to see if I was the same person. There was such a glory over everything; the sun came like gold through the trees, and over the fields, and I felt like I was in Heaven."[4] But this feeling of joy didn't last long.

She was unhappy. "There was no one to welcome me to the land of freedom. I was a stranger in a strange land; and my home, after all, was down in Maryland; because my father, my mother, my brothers, and sisters, and friends were there. But I was free, and they should be free,"[5] Araminta explained. She immediately set her mind on a crusade. She quickly found work in various hotels and private homes as a cook and servant. Every penny was saved with the intent of using her money to rescue all her family members.

It didn't take long for her to act. In December 1850, when she heard news that her niece Kessiah was about to be put on the auction block, Araminta returned to Dorchester County, Maryland, at once and made the rescue. On her second expedition, she rescued her brother Moses and two other men. In the autumn 1851, Araminta embarked on a third mission to convince her husband to reunite with her in the North. But her hopes were soon dashed. She found out that he had married another woman. Even more heartbreaking, he refused to go see her. Although she was devastated, Araminta salvaged her mission by leading a group of slaves to Philadelphia.

Her initial successes and strong faith in God gave her the courage and confidence to sustain her crusade. But it was her ingenuity and foresight that made her rescue efforts successful time after time. To lessen the chance of detection, she organized her escapes during winter when daylight was short. Escapes began on Saturday evenings because newspaper advertisements on fugitives couldn't be taken out until Monday. This gave the fugitives a two-day head start. Araminta sang spiritual songs with secret messages to warn her group of impending danger. She paid men to follow bounty hunters and tear down their reward postings. She carried a pistol for protection as well as for ensuring the success of the mission. On one occasion, a fugitive had second thoughts and wanted to retreat. "You go on or die,"[6] she threatened, with her gun pointing to his head. Several days later, he was a freed man.

The success of each mission depended heavily on friends who provided food and shelter at strategic locations along the way. Sometimes, she got donations from sympathetic supporters who helped finance her operations. For eleven years, Araminta risked her life again and again while conducting nineteen missions in all on her runaway train on the Underground Railroad. Not one passenger was lost.

Araminta rescued many people from slavery and nearly all of her family members. Who was this selfless crusader?

HARRIET TUBMAN

For Harriet Tubman, freedom by itself did not bring her happiness. She found happiness by leading her family and friends to freedom.

Harriet Tubman's Bio

Birth Name: Araminta Ross
Birthplace: Dorchester County, Maryland
Birth Date: circa 1820
Died: March 10, 1913
Age: Ninety-three years old

Achievements

Led over three hundred Negroes to freedom

Served as nurse and spy for the Union during the Civil War

SELECTED QUOTES BY HARRIET TUBMAN

"There was one of two things I had a right to: liberty or death; if I could not have one, I would have the other."

"On my Underground Railroad, I never run off the track and I never lost a passenger."

"Slavery is the next thing to hell."

FURTHER READING

Harriet Tubman: The Road to Freedom by Catherine Clinton
Harriet Tubman: Imagining a Life by Beverly Lowry
Bound for the Promised Land: Harriet Tubman, Portrait of an American Hero by Kate Clifford Larson

AL MIGHTY

Al always had a curious mind.

As a child, he experimented with fire and accidentally burned the family barn to the ground. Had there been a strong wind, the whole town might have been reduced to ashes. Dad punished his son with a public whipping in the town square.

Naturally, his mischief carried over to school. After only three months, he came home in tears because the teacher had called him a problem child. Mom quickly came to his aid. "I found out what a good thing a mother was. She brought me back to the school and angrily told the teacher that he didn't know what he was talking about. I determined right then and there that I would be worthy of her, and show her that her confidence had not been misplaced,"[1] Al said.

The family was chronically in debt. During winter, Al frequently came down with colds, earaches, bronchitis, and other illnesses. The combination of unpaid tuition and excessive absences put an end to his formal schooling at age twelve. When Al wasn't enrolled in school, his mom gave lessons and taught him reading, writing, and arithmetic.

One day, Mom presented her nine-year-old son with a physical science book that contained details of various experiments that could be performed at home. He carried out every one of the experiments in that book in his bedroom. He created such a mess in his bedroom that his mom ordered him to use the cellar as his laboratory. Dad was more concerned about safety. "He will blow us all up!"[2] Dad worried. As always, Mom defended her son. "Let him be," she said. "Al knows what he's about."[3]

By thirteen, Al decided to help support the family, so he persuaded his mom to let him take the job of selling newspapers and candies aboard a train traveling daily from home in Port Huron to Detroit, Michigan. The days were long. The train left Port Huron at 7 AM daily for the more than three-hour ride to Detroit. Then, there would be a six-hour stopover in Detroit before the train returned home at 9:30 PM. Each night, Al came home and gave his mother a dollar from his earnings.

During the layovers, he pursued his love of learning instilled by his mom. He spent many hours reading at the Detroit library. "I started with the first book on the bottom shelf and went through the lot, one by one. I didn't read a few books. I read the library,"[4] Al said. At other times, he stayed aboard the stationary train and conducted experiments in his makeshift chemistry lab.

By sixteen, he decided it was time to learn a trade. Telegraphy was the most advanced form of communication in the 1860s. Messages were coded as a series of dots and dashes that were sent over the wire. There was great demand for telegraphers, and the pay was good.

One day in late summer 1862, Al rescued a three-year-old boy who was playing on the track of an oncoming train. As a show of gratitude for saving his son, the father offered to teach Al to become a telegrapher. After five months of training, he gained enough knowledge to land a part-time job. But Al's restless mind wouldn't allow him to settle in one place.

During the next six years, he hopped from one telegraph office to the next, from city to city, picking up valuable knowledge and new ideas along the way. He read constantly and invented things to solve all kinds of problems that confronted him, everywhere he went. Once, he created a device that slowed down the incoming telegraphs so that he could translate the message into words at his own pace. Another time, Al got tired of sharing his room with rats so he invented a device that immediately electrocuted them as soon as they came in contact with it.

Al's knack for inventing things and his constant love of learning soon gave him the necessary confidence and skills to change his career to inventor. His first patent on an electric vote recorder, a device intended to speed the voting process was a commercial failure. But this didn't stop him. He went on to make improvements on the telegraph and the telephone. His invention of the phonograph, a device that records and plays back sound, brought him international fame. But he is best remembered for another invention.

Up until the late 1800s, gas lamps were used to light homes and buildings. Although the first incandescent light was created by Humphry Davy in 1802, it would take another seventy-five years before the light bulb was made bright enough with a long enough life-span to be practical. Scores of inventors worked on the light bulb, but none succeeded, including Al. In the autumn of 1877, he made a number of attempts at making a practical light bulb but stopped working on it when he encountered too many challenges.

Then on September 8, 1878, when Al saw inventor William Wallace working on his arc lights, a different way of creating light versus a light bulb, he just had to give another try. "I believe I can beat you making electric lights. I don't think you are working in the right direction,"[5] he challenged Wallace. For the first time, Al understood what it took to make a practical light bulb. In theory, all that was needed was a thin, durable filament placed inside a tight vacuum-sealed glass bulb. Then electricity had to be run through the filament to heat it to a high enough temperature without melting it and light would appear. In practice, however, this proved to be Al's greatest challenge.

Al began experimenting with the filament. First, he tried using carbon because of its high melting point. But carbon was fragile and lasted for only a few minutes. Next, he used platinum, which created a brilliant light, but under high heat the metal quickly melted and the light went out after a few minutes. Meanwhile, his investors wanted to see results. The added pressure forced Al and his staff to double their efforts.

By January 1879, the latest batch of light bulbs showed encouraging results as the platinum filament burned for over an hour. He kept experimenting with different metals and materials, producing filaments of different thicknesses, size, and shapes. Some were too fragile and broke before they were inserted into the bulbs. Others burned out once electricity passed through them. But he never gave up. "I never quit until I get what I'm after. Negative results are just what I'm after. They are just as valuable to me as positive results,"[6] he said. So he continued his search for a more durable filament and an apparatus to create a better vacuum inside the glass bulbs.

When Al wasn't conducting experiments, he was reading scientific journals to learn and get new ideas. By fall 1879, Al had obtained a new air pump, which enabled him to produce an almost ideal vacuum inside the bulbs. He had learned about the new air pump from one of his scientific journals.

With half the problem solved, he returned to his first instinct of using carbon for the filament. By using a combination of cotton thread and carbon molded into a hairpin shape, then baked for a number of hours, the desired filament was made. Finally, after a year and a half, after countless hours, after three thousand trials using sixteen hundred different materials, the moment of truth arrived.

It was the evening of October 21, 1878. Al turned on the electricity, and the bulb illuminated as expected. As the electricity increased, the bulb still burned, even brighter. It burned for many hours. "I think we've got it,"[7] Al said. "If it can burn forty hours, I can make it last a hundred."[8] No matter what project Al worked on, he applied the same kind of tireless effort. He put in sixteen to eighteen hours a day in the lab. In the end, Al had 1,093 inventions credited to his name.

Al's inventions brightened the world in many ways. Who was this most famous inventor?

THOMAS EDISON

As the most prolific inventor in history, Thomas Edison succeeded because he dared to fail and learned from his failures. Great inventions are often the result of persistence and hard work.

Thomas Edison's Bio

Birth Name: Thomas Alva Edison
Birthplace: Milan, Ohio, United States
Birth Date: February 11, 1847
Died: October 18, 1931
Age: Eighty-four years old

Achievements

Total of 1,093 patents

Automobile	8
Battery	141
Cement	40
Electric Light and Power	389
Electric Pen and Mimeograph	5
Miscellaneous	35
Motion Pictures	9
Ore Separator	62
Phonograph	195
Railroad	25
Telegraph	150
Telephone	34

Selected Quotes by Thomas Edison

"Genius is 1 percent inspiration and 99 percent perspiration."

"I never quit until I get what I'm after. Negative results are just what I'm after. They are just as valuable to me as positive results."

"I'll never give up for I may have a streak of luck before I die."

"The man who doesn't make up his mind to cultivate the habit of thinking misses the greatest pleasures in life."

"The brain that isn't used rusts."

"Any other bright-minded fellow can accomplish just as much if he will stick like hell and remember nothing that's any good works by itself. You got to *make* the damn thing work."

"Opportunity is missed by most people because it is dressed in overalls and looks like work."

"I have not failed. I've just found ten thousand ways that won't work."

"Many of life's failures are people who did not realize how close they were to success when they gave up."

"If we all did the things we are capable of doing, we would literally astound ourselves."

"If I find ten thousand ways something won't work, I haven't failed. I am not discouraged, because every wrong attempt discarded is another step forward."

"A genius is just a talented person who does his homework."

Further Reading

Edison by Mathew Josephson
A Streak of Luck by Robert E. Conot
Edison: The Man Who Made the Future by Ronald W. Clark

HEART OF GOLD

Her father was poisoned to death when Agnes was only eight years old.

The sudden loss of the breadwinner brought tremendous grief and financial hardship to the family. After a brief period, Mom summoned all her strength to meet the needs of her three children by taking up tailoring and selling fabric. But even under these difficult times, Mom continued the family tradition of sharing with the poor. No matter what, she always made room at the family table for strangers and friends and made sure no one left empty-handed. Sometimes Mom made house calls to the poor by bringing food and taking care of them. Young Agnes tagged along on many such occasions and, in time, learned the virtues of generosity, kindness, and compassion. "When you do good," Mom instructed, "do it quietly, as if you were throwing a stone into the sea."[1]

From a very early age, Agnes attended church regularly. As the years passed, her mother and Catholicism formed an ever-greater influence on her. "I was only twelve years old when I first felt the desire to become a nun,"[2] Agnes recalled. At first, her mother objected to the idea. After all, Agnes was still a child. But mother and daughter continued to spend many hours in church. Agnes even went after school to participate in church activities.

One day, she became inspired when she learned about the missionaries' work with the poor in India. By the time she was eighteen, she was convinced of her calling in life. A month after her eighteenth birthday, Agnes waved a tearful goodbye to her mother at the train station. It was the last time she ever saw her.

She arrived at the doorsteps of Loreto Abbey in Rathfarnham, Ireland, for her training to become a missionary. There, she focused on learning English, the official language of communication. After seven weeks of religious studies and training, Agnes set sail for India on December 1, 1928. Shortly upon her arrival in Calcutta, she was sent to Darjeeling to begin the intensive two-year training program taught by Loreto nuns.

Right away, Agnes assumed her duties with enthusiasm. After her training, Agnes began teaching in the Loreto convent school in Darjeeling. Later, she was sent to Loreto Entally, a school in Calcutta where she taught geography and history.

On May 24, 1937, in Darjeeling, Agnes officially became a Loreto nun when she took her three vows: poverty, chastity, and obedience. Everything was going well. "This is a new life. Our center here is very fine. I am a teacher, and I love the work. I am also Head of the whole school, and everybody wishes me well,"[3] she wrote her mother. In response, Mom sent a harsh reminder: "Do not forget that you went to India for the sake of the poor."[4]

Agnes had made visits every Sunday to visit the poor in the bustees, the slums of Calcutta, but thus far had done little to help them. Then on a fateful day, on September 10, 1946, Agnes received a momentous spiritual calling. "I was to leave the convent and help the poor while living among them. It was an order. To fail it would have been to break the faith,"[5] she remembered. As ideas formed, Agnes wrote them down on slips of paper. She was to start a new congregation that would be dedicated solely to help the poorest of the poor.

After a year of waiting, she was granted permission by her superiors to leave Loreto and try her experiment for one year. After several weeks of medical training in a hospital, she went to the slums. "To leave Loreto was my greatest sacrifice, the most difficult thing I have ever done,"[6] Agnes later confessed. "It was much more difficult than to leave my family and country to enter religious life. Loreto, my spiritual training, my work there, meant everything to me."[7]

In December 1948, Agnes got permission to open a "school" in one of the slums in Motijhil. Out in the open, Agnes taught the children the Bengali alphabet by writing the letters in the dirt using a stick while the children squatted. Still, the class size of twenty-one students on the first day nearly doubled on the following day. As word spread about Agnes' work, people gave her money and offered help.

Agnes rented two huts in Motijhil for five rupees each. One served as a school. The other hut served as the first home for the sick and dying. From early morning until late in the evening, Agnes filled each day by teaching children, tending to the sick, the elderly, and the homeless, and bringing comfort to Muslim and Hindu families living in the slums. To gain the trust and respect of the poor, Agnes wore a white sari made of the cheapest cloth and maintained a plain diet. Day after day, she kept to her busy schedule. "When I am in the work, looking at the hundreds of suffering, I think of nothing but them and I am really very happy,"[8] she said.

However, there were times, especially during the first few months, when she felt lonely and had doubts about her mission. After all, the success of her mission was totally dependent on the generosity of others. But she persevered, and rewards came her way. In February 1949, Agnes moved into her new convent in Creek Lane. A gentleman had permitted Agnes to use one of his apartments free of charge. At times when Agnes went hungry, the landlord gave her food upon request.

A few weeks later, her loneliness was no more. Subhasini Das, a Bengali girl who had been one of Agnes's pupils at the Loreto convent school in Entally, joined her mission. Then more of her former pupils arrived. To each one of her missionaries, she stressed on helping the poorest of the poor because no one cared for them. One evening, Agnes picked up a dying woman lying in the street and took her to the home. "So I did for her all that my love can do. I put her in bed, and there was such a beautiful smile on her face. She took hold of my hand, as she said one word only: 'thank you' and she died,"[9] Agnes recalled. On another occasion, she and her missionaries brought home a man from the sewer, half-eaten by worms. The grateful man spoke, "I have lived like an animal in the street, but I am going to die like an angel, loved and cared for."[10] "It was so wonderful to see the greatness of that man who could speak like that, who could die like that without blaming anybody, without cursing at anybody, without comparing anything,"[11] Agnes said.

One by one, Agnes taught her missionaries how to provide care for the sick and dying, how to beg for donations, and how to teach children. As her work gained more and more publicity, donations came pouring in and more doctors, nurses, and other professionals volunteered their services. Young women by the thousands took their vows and followed her footsteps.

She worked tirelessly for more than sixty years. To all those people she helped, she was like a mother to them. Who was this truly selfless humanitarian?

MOTHER TERESA

Mother Teresa's life-long sacrifice and devotion to helping the poorest of the poor is a testament to the power of love for all humankind, regardless of religion, ethnicity, race, sex, disability, or status.

MOTHER TERESA'S BIO

Birth Name: Agnes Gonxha Bojaxhiu
Birthplace: Skopje, Republic of Macedonia (formerly Albania)
Birth Date: August 26, 1910
Died: September 5, 1997
Age: Eighty-seven years old

ACHIEVEMENTS AND AWARDS

She received the Nobel Peace Prize in 1979.

Over the years, her charity network called the Missionaries of Charity expanded around the world with centers devoted to serving the "poorest of the poor." By 1996, she was operating over five hundred missions in more than one hundred countries.

Selected Quotes by Mother Teresa

"Kindness is a language we all understand. Even the blind can see it and the deaf can hear it."

"It is not how much we do, but how much love we put in the doing. It is not how much we give, but how much love we put in the giving."

"Let us not be satisfied with just giving money. Money is not enough, money can be got, but they need your hearts to love them. So, spread your love everywhere you go."

"If you judge people, you have no time to love them."

"The poor give us much more than we give them. They're such strong people, living day to day with no food, and they never curse, never complain. We don't have to give them pity or sympathy. We have so much to learn from them."

"Love is doing small things with great love."

"Do not wait for leaders. Do it alone, person to person."

"Let no one ever come to you without leaving better and happier."

"Kind words can be short and easy to speak, but their echoes are truly endless."

"If you can't feed a hundred people, then feed just one."

"The fruit of love is service. The fruit of service is peace."

"If there are poor on the moon, we shall go there too."

FURTHER READING

Mother Teresa: The Authorized Biography by Navin Chawla
Mother Teresa: In My Own Words by Mother Teresa
Mother Teresa: A Complete Authorized Biography by Kathryn Spink

Stand and Deliver

One day, Michael's friend told him that they couldn't play together anymore. When he asked his parents for an explanation, he learned for the first time the issue of racial discrimination. The six-year-old sat at the dinner table and listened as his parents recounted some of the tragedies that had taken place and some of the insults they had encountered.

"I was greatly shocked," Michael said, "and from that moment on I was determined to hate every white person."[1] But his parents always told him that he should not hate the white man because it was his duty as a Christian to love him. Still, their reasoning didn't seem logical. "How could I love a race of people who hated me and who had been responsible for breaking me up with one of my best childhood friends?"[2] he asked. This question puzzled Michael for a number of years.

By the time he was eight years old, Michael had experienced racial discrimination firsthand. One day, at a downtown store, a white lady slapped him and then accused him of stepping on her foot, using a racial slur. Michael didn't dare retaliate. Later on, when Michael was fourteen, another incident took place as he was returning home on a bus from an oratory contest he had just won. That night, the white bus driver ordered Michael and his teacher to give up their seats to some white passengers who had just boarded. When the two of them didn't act quickly enough, the driver began cursing them. Michael became furious and didn't want to get up. But Mrs. Bradley convinced him to do so because that was the law. "That night will never leave my memory. It was the angriest I have ever been in my life,"[3] Michael recalled.

By the time he entered Morehouse College at fifteen, he was very much aware of the numerous injustices affecting his people. His college professors encouraged him to find a solution to the racial problems. Right away, he started working with organizations that were pushing for civil rights and equality. While working with the Intercollegiate Council, Michael saw many white people, particularly among the younger generation, working for the same cause. Gradually, his initial resentment of white people subsided as his appreciation for their cooperation grew.

As time passed, Michael became more and more involved in political and social reform. "I could envision myself playing a part in breaking down the legal barriers to Negro rights,"[4] he said. Since high school, he had felt a sense of duty to serve humanity, primarily because his father, grandfather, and great-grandfather were preachers. Before, he thought about studying medicine or law, but now his mission in life was clear. "I felt a sense of responsibility I could not escape,"[5] he said.

After graduating from college, this nineteen-year-old entered Crozer Seminary on a quest to eliminate social evil. Here, he spent a great deal of time studying the social and philosophical theories of great philosophers from Plato to Gandhi. After reading Gandhi's work, Michael learned that nonviolent resistance was one of the most potent weapons against oppression.

It didn't take long before this new arsenal was put into battle. On December 1, 1955, a woman by the name of Rosa Parks was arrested for refusing to give up her seat on the bus to a white man. This event sparked the beginning of the civil rights movement in Montgomery, Alabama. That night, Jo Ann Robinson, a civil rights activist and professor, initiated her plans for a one-day boycott. With the help of her students, she printed and distributed thousands of pamphlets urging blacks to stay off the city buses on Monday, December 5.

The next night, a group of ministers and community leaders met at Michael's church to discuss the idea of boycott. After some debate, the consensus was to support the boycott and spread the word in church on Sunday.

Early Monday morning, one bus after another with only white passengers inside passed Michael's house. During the rush hours, the sidewalks were crowded with laborers walking proudly to their jobs and home again. Some walked for as many as twelve miles. "A miracle had taken place,"[6] Michael said. The day after the boycott, a new organization, the Montgomery Improvement Association (MIA) was formed to decide on the future of the boycott. Without hesitation, Michael was elected unanimously as the leader. His wife showed equal support. "You know that whatever you do," she said quietly, "you have my backing."[7]

While Michael and his organization were using diplomacy to repeal the bus segregation laws with city hall, the whites used numerous schemes to break the boycott. Black cab drivers were prohibited from charging the same ten-cent fare as the bus fare. They were forced to charge the minimum forty-five-cent fare. As a result, the end of the cheap cab rides posed a huge potential problem for thousands of blacks who had no other way to get to work.

With military-like speed and precision, the MIA responded with its own "taxi" service. Blacks who owned cars picked up and dropped off passengers at specific locations. In desperation, the whites turned to threats and violence. By the middle of January, the number of threatening phone calls and letters Michael received had risen to forty a day. His home was bombed on January 30, 1956. Luckily, no one was injured.

When violence failed to work, the opposition resorted to mass arrests. On February 21, 1956, Michael and over a hundred of his followers were indicted under an old anti-boycott law. Even though he was away during the indictments, he quickly returned to join his friends who were already in jail. His father and family friends warned him about his safety, but he chose to follow his conscience. "I must go back to Montgomery. It would be the height of cowardice for me to stay away. I would rather be in jail ten years than desert my people now. I have begun the struggle, and I can't turn back. I have reached the point of no return,"[8] Michael explained.

Throughout this whole ordeal, his wife, Coretta, backed him every step of the way. "She was always strong and courageous. In the darkest moments, she always brought the light of hope. I am convinced that if I had not a wife with the fortitude, strength, and calmness of Corrie, I could not have withstood the ordeals and tensions surrounding the movement."[9] Michael said. Despite all the attacks, Michael urged his followers to stay off the buses and never retaliate with force.

It worked. On November 13, 1956, the U.S. Supreme Court declared segregation on buses unconstitutional. The Montgomery Bus Boycott, which lasted 381 days, was officially over. This victory gave Michael the courage and momentum to continue the fight for his people. He fought tirelessly, gallantly, and peacefully all the way to the end, all because of a dream he had.

This eloquent orator united his people in their struggle for civil rights. Who was this great American civil rights leader?

MARTIN LUTHER KING JR.

Martin Luther King Jr. always practiced what he preached. He fought against racial injustice and poverty using nonviolent means.

Martin Luther King Jr.'s Bio

Birth Name: Michael King Jr. (His name was changed by his
                 father at age six.)
Birthplace: Atlanta, Georgia, United States
Birth Date: January 15, 1929
Died: April 4, 1968
Age: Thirty-nine years old

Achievements and Awards

1963:   Led the famous march to Washington, DC, where he
        delivered his "I Have a Dream" speech

1964:   Received Nobel Peace Prize

1977:   Awarded Presidential Medal of Freedom (posthumous)

1986:   Martin Luther King Jr. Day was established as a U.S.
        national holiday

2004:   Awarded Congressional Gold Medal (posthumous)

SELECTED QUOTES BY MARTIN LUTHER KING JR.

"Nothing worthwhile is gained without sacrifice."

"The quality, not the longevity, of one's life is what is important."

"The thing that we need in the world today is a group of men and women who will stand up for right and be opposed to wrong, wherever it is."

"The believer in nonviolence is the person who will willingly allow himself to be the victim of violence but will never inflict violence upon another."

"The ultimate test of a man is not where he stands in moments of comfort and moments of convenience, but where he stands in moments of challenge and moments of controversy."

"A productive and happy life is not something you find; it is something you make."

"I would rather be a man of conviction than a man of conformity. Occasionally, in life one develops a conviction so precious and meaningful that he will stand on it till the end. This is what I have found in nonviolence."

"Hate is just as injurious to the hater as it is to the hated. Like an unchecked cancer, hate corrodes the personality and eats away its vital unity. Many of our inner conflicts are rooted in hate. This is why the psychiatrists say, "Love or perish." Hate is too great a burden to bear."

"Like life, racial understanding is not something that we find but something that we must create."

"If you have never found something so dear and so precious to you that you will die for it, then you aren't fit to live. You died when you refused to stand up for right. You died when you refused to stand up for truth. You died when you refused to stand up for justice ..."

"We must learn to live together as brothers or perish together as fools."

"Let no man pull you low enough to hate him."

"Hatred paralyzes life; love releases it. Hatred confuses life; love harmonizes it. Hatred darkens life; love illuminates it."

"Our lives begin to end the day we become silent about things that matter."

"Injustice anywhere is a threat to justice everywhere."

"One who condones evils is just as guilty as the one who perpetrates it."

FURTHER READING

Martin Luther King, Jr.: A Life by Marshall Frady
The Autobiography of Martin Luther King Jr. by Martin Luther King
The Martin Luther King Jr. Companion: Quotations from the Speeches, Essays, and Books of Martin Luther King Jr. by Martin Luther King

HAVE NO FEAR

By the age of ten, both of her parents were dead.

Just before Anna's eighth birthday, her twenty-nine-year-old mother contracted diphtheria and died. In her will, Mom gave custody of her children to her mother. Anna's father was a delusional alcoholic who had been exiled from home. A few months later, tragedy struck again. Anna's three-year-old brother shared their mother's fate. Then a little over a year later, her father slipped into a coma from a fall and died.

Both of her parents belonged to New York's upper-class. Anna, the firstborn child, was a bitter disappointment to her mother from the start. "You have no looks, so see to it that you have manners,"[1] Mom criticized. "In the beginning, because I felt, as only a young girl can feel it, all the pain of being an ugly duckling, I was not only timid, I was afraid,"[2] Anna confessed. Nothing she did met Mom's approval. Dad, on the other hand, called her "a miracle from Heaven." "With my father I was perfectly happy,"[3] Anna said.

As orphans, Anna and her brother, Hall, made their permanent home at Grandma's house in Manhattan, New York. There, Anna continued to attend classes taught by a private tutor. For years, she craved the two things that were missing in her life: attention and admiration. "I would have given anything to be a singer,"[4] she said.

By the time she was fifteen, Grandma sent her overseas to Allenswood, a private girls' school near London. The three years she spent over there turned out to be the happiest of her life. "This was the first time in my life that my fears left me. If I lived up to the rules and told the truth, there was nothing to fear,"[5] Anna said.

Under Marie Souvestre's guidance and tender, loving care, Anna gradually developed into a confident and independent young thinker. Her teacher had changed her life. By eighteen, Anna had to return home to assume the traditional role of a debutante, a young woman making her formal entrance into society. It was customary for debutantes to attend parties and mingle with other wealthy young men and women. Once again, her insecurities about her looks made her feel uneasy at formal gatherings.

Being a debutante provided Anna with at least one benefit. She enjoyed being a member of the Junior League, an organization of wealthy young women that served the poor. Anna volunteered as a teacher of calisthenics and fancy dancing to children living in slums. Later, she joined the Consumers' League and investigated on the working conditions of young female workers in garment factories and department stores.

At nineteen, Anna had learned a great deal about the lower-class in society. It was at this time that she began dating a distant cousin named Franklin. Two years later, they were married.

In the early of 1900s, it was customary for a woman to stay home and support her husband's ambitions. Things were going well for the married couple until the autumn of 1909. Then tragedy struck. The couple's third child, Franklin Jr., at seven months old, came down with the flu and died.

By the time Anna turned twenty-six, her husband decided to enter politics. She stood firmly by his side with the couple's three children. Even though she was consumed with household duties, she found the time for volunteer work. During World War I, Anna became one of seventy thousand women volunteers at Red Cross canteens handing out soup and sandwiches to servicemen at the railroad stations. After the war, she spent several days a week visiting wounded soldiers at a veteran's hospital.

With Franklin in public service, Anna felt the need to be more independent so that she could help his career. So, she enrolled in a business school and took courses in shorthand and typing. A few years later, another tragedy struck the family. One afternoon in August 1921, Franklin was stricken with polio, which paralyzed him from the waist down. The couple emerged from this ordeal stronger and more determined than ever before.

While her husband was adjusting to his handicap, Anna became active in the women's division of the State Democratic Committee to keep Franklin's political interests alive. But as much as she enjoyed meeting people and doing volunteer work, she was fearful of public speaking. She was so worried about how others would perceive her that her voice trembled as she spoke. A family friend offered her this advice: "Have something to say, say it, and then sit down."⁶ Little by little, her confidence in her speaking abilities improved. As her reputation grew, newspapers, magazines, and radio stations called on her to share her viewpoints.

At that time, Anna's beliefs were only supported by a small number of female social activists. Like her fellow reformers, she pushed for a number of equal rights for women: a forty-eight-hour work week, a fair minimum wage, the end of child labor, the right to organize into trade unions, and an equal voice in government.

Over time, Anna developed enough courage to tackle her challenges head on without fear. As a girl, Anna had been afraid of the water. Now, this forty-year-old mother decided to take swimming lessons so she could teach her boys. When her husband became president, she went against tradition by holding regular press conferences to only female reporters. Because women reporters were losing their jobs, Anna used this ploy to protect them from being fired.

As the first lady, she went wherever she chose and refused to use the service of a limousine, a police escort, or Secret Service agents. "No one's going to hurt me," she said, "I simply can't imagine being afraid of going among Americans as I always have, as I always shall."⁷ She went all over the country to give lectures and raised many of the issues that were facing blacks and minorities, the homeless, and the unemployed.

However, not everyone appreciated Anna's efforts for social justice. Some people, including government officials, were offended by her actions and political views. "I wish that Anna would stick to her knitting and keep out airs of the affairs connected with my department,"⁸ Interior Secretary Harold Ickes denounced. She politely responded by saying, "Everyone must live their own life in their own way and not according to anybody else's ideas."⁹

In 1939, Anna defied segregation laws when she sat between whites and blacks at the Southern Conference for Human Welfare in Birmingham, Alabama. Four years later, the fifty-nine-year-old first lady visited American troops in many war zones in the South Pacific to boost morale. She flew around the world many times meeting heads of state as a goodwill ambassador and served as a delegate to the United Nations. She worked tirelessly to the end, regardless of what people said. "Having learned to stare down fear, I long ago reached the point where there is no living person whom I fear, and few challenges that I am not willing to face."[10]

Richard Lam

Anna was the most loved and influential woman of her time. Who
was this devoted human rights activist?

ELEANOR ROOSEVELT

Eleanor Roosevelt confronted each one of her fears and conquered them. She did the things she thought she could not do.

ELEANOR ROOSEVELT'S BIO

Birth Name: Anna Eleanor Roosevelt
Birthplace: New York, New York, United States
Birth Date: October 11, 1884
Died: November 7, 1962
Age: Seventy-eight years old

ACHIEVEMENTS

She supported many worthy causes, especially for women and African Americans, notably the Tuskegee Airmen, who were the first black combat pilots.

In 1945, she served as a delegate to the United Nations General Assembly under U.S. President Harry S. Truman.

She helped draft the *United Nations Universal Declaration of Human Rights*. She served as the first chairperson of the United Nations Human Rights Commission. The declaration was adopted by the United Nations General Assembly on December 10, 1948.

Selected Quotes by Eleanor Roosevelt

"You gain strength, courage, and confidence by every experience in which you really stop to look fear in the face. You are able to say to yourself, 'I have lived through this horror. I can take the next thing that comes along.' You must do the thing you think you cannot do."

"People grow through experience if they meet life honestly and courageously. This is how character is built."

"The future belongs to those who believe in the beauty of their dreams."

"Anyone who has gone through great suffering is bound to have a greater sympathy and understanding of the problems of mankind."

"You have no security unless you can live bravely, excitingly, imaginatively; unless you can choose a challenge instead of a competence."

"Learn from the mistakes of others. You can't live long enough to make them all yourself."

"Life was meant to be lived, and curiosity must be kept alive. One must never, for whatever reason, turn his back on life."

"One thing life has taught me: if you are interested, you never have to look for new interests. They come to you. When you are genuinely interested in one thing, it will always lead to something else."

"The purpose of life is to live it, to taste experience to the utmost, to reach out eagerly and without fear for newer and richer experience."

"Great minds discuss ideas; average minds discuss events; small minds discuss people."

"It is not fair to ask of others what you are unwilling to do yourself."

"Justice cannot be for one side alone, but must be for both."

"No one can make you feel inferior without your consent."

"If you lose money you lose much,
If you lose friends you lose more,
If you lose faith you lose all."

"Never be bored, and you will never be boring."

"No man is defeated without until he is defeated within."

"Do the things that interest you and do them with all your heart. Don't be concerned about whether people are watching you or criticizing you. The chances are that they aren't paying attention to you."

"Make up your mind to live as happily and as fully as you can. Seize on everything that comes your way which makes life more interesting, or agreeable."

"I am convinced that every effort must be made in childhood to teach the young to use their own minds. For one thing is sure: If they don't make up their minds, someone will do it for them."

"All of life is a constant education."

"Example is the best lesson there is."

"If you fail the first time then you'll just have to try harder the second time. After all, there's no real reason why you should fail. Just stop thinking about yourself."

"The answer to fear is not to cower and hide; it is not to surrender feebly without contest. The answer is to stand and face it boldly. Look at it, analyze it, and in the end, act. With action, confidence grows."

"One of the most effective techniques in dealing with people is to appeal to them for their help. If they think you are in need of their assistance and that you will appreciate it, they are apt to do their best to help your need."

"We must join in an effort to use all knowledge for the good of all human beings. When we do that we shall have nothing to fear."

FURTHER READING

The Autobiography of Eleanor Roosevelt by Eleanor Roosevelt
Eleanor Roosevelt: A Life of Discovery by Russell Freedman
Courage in a Dangerous World: The Political Writings of Eleanor Roosevelt by Allida M. Black

FOLLOW YOUR PASSION

His first word was "piz."

When the baby demanded, "Piz, piz," the mother gave her son a *lapiz* or a pencil. With the pencil in hand, baby Pablo was then able to tell his parents what he wanted simply by drawing them on paper.

At four, he used his creative imagination to project animals and flowers on a wall from the paper figures he cut out. Each time his two older cousins made a request, Pablo would produce, as if by magic, the exact drawing or cut-out that was asked for.

From the beginning, he was a restless child and never liked to follow the rules. So, naturally school was never a pleasant experience for him. The family maid had to drag him to school, but he threw such terrible tantrums that his parents sent him to a private school. But even that didn't help. He still paid little attention to his teachers. "It's incredible," he recalled later, "I stared at the clock like an idiot, eyes raised, head sideways …"[1] Sometimes, he would go to the window and just watch people along the street stroll by. "Don't think I didn't try," Pablo said, "I tried hard to concentrate."[2]

But no matter how hard he tried, the three Rs, reading, writing, and arithmetic, were always difficult to master. Especially in arithmetic, he never quite understood the rules or concepts with numbers. To him, numbers represented only pictures, like the number seven was nothing but a nose drawn upside down.

In October 1891, the ten-year-old and his family moved to Corunna, Spain, where his father, Don Jose, landed a new job as a drawing teacher. There, Pablo continued to doodle away, filling the margin of his books with sketches of people and animals. His disobedience usually led to confinement in a detention room that had whitewashed walls and benches. "I loved it when they sent me there, because I could take a pad of paper and draw nonstop,"[3] he said.

Recognizing his son's artistic talent, Don Jose decided that it was best for his son to begin formal training at an art school. At Da Guarda Institute where Dad taught, Pablo first sat in his father's ornamental drawing class. From his drawings, it was clear that Pablo had an exceptional combination of eye-hand coordination and a sharp eye for detail. The grades given by his teachers usually varied from "excellent" to "excellent with honorable mention."

When he got home, Pablo received additional instruction from Dad. "My father cut off the feet of a dead pigeon," Pablo remembered. "He pinned them to a board in proper position, and I copied them in detail until he was satisfied."[4] Before long, the son was painting the feet of the pigeons on his father's oil canvases.

While he continued to hone his skills as an artist, a tragedy occurred that would leave a deep emotional scar in Pablo. In January 1895, his eight-year-old sister, Conchita, died of diphtheria. About the same time, Pablo's father mysteriously gave him his paint brushes and swore never to paint again.

Hoping to improve his family life, Dad sought a job transfer to Barcelona. There, Pablo's enrollment at the Barcelona School of Fine Arts proved to be a waste of time. He felt the instruction stifled his creativity and artistic vision. "I detest that period of my studies in Barcelona,"[5] he said. To make matters worse, Dad's sharp criticism and unsolicited advice often created tension between father and son.

On the other hand, his mother's unconditional support was more soothing for his ears. "If you become a soldier," she told him, "you will be a general. If you become a priest, you'll end up as the Pope!"[6] But as far as being an artist, Pablo had little to show for his artistic talents. Very few of his paintings were sold. His painting titled *The First Communion* received only a lukewarm reception at the Exhibition of Fine Arts in Barcelona in April 1896. Finally, a year later, his *Science and Charity* finally brought him some recognition, an honorable mention at the General Fine Arts Exhibition in Madrid. Uncle Don Salvador was so impressed by the painting that he immediately gathered all the relatives for contributions to send the young talented artist to the most prestigious art school in Spain.

In the fall of 1897, the sixteen-year-old arrived at the Royal Academy of San Fernando in Madrid. Once again he became frustrated with the school's curriculum and rigid ways. When his uncle learned about

Pablo's lack of productivity and excessive absenteeism, he immediately cut off financial aid. Pablo had to survive with what little money his parents could send. Too poor to rent a studio, he was forced to paint outdoors.

On February 1, 1900, Pablo held his first exhibition at Els Quatre Gats, a cabaret in Barcelona. No success. An anonymous review criticized his work for exhibiting "unevenness," "carelessness," and "outside influences." Such criticisms made him more frustrated with the art world in Spain. He dreamt of going to Paris where aspiring artists went to learn from the works of old masters such as Lautrec, Renoir, and the Impressionists, and contemporaries like Cezanne and Gauguin. Again, his parents made the financial sacrifice and bought him a round-trip train ticket to Paris.

Just before leaving for Paris, the nineteen-year-old would do a self-portrait with a bold title that would one day fittingly describe his status in the art world. He signed it "Yo, el Rey" three times as a show of strong self-confidence: "I, the King; I, the King; I, the King."[7]

It took a period of time for Pablo to get acclimated with Parisian life. He didn't speak French, but he did find company among a small group of Spanish artists pursuing their dreams just like him. He spent many hours in museums and contemporary art galleries studying the masterpieces as well as the paintings in the latest style. Afterward, he returned to his fresh canvases with many new ideas, which he incorporated into his unique style.

Still, very few paintings sold. The main reason was that almost all of his paintings portrayed the dark side of humanity. His blue-colored canvases were often filled with beggars, overburdened mothers, and sick people. But he never gave up despite the little success and the tough working conditions. He continued to paint without heat in his studio during the winter. And in the summer, the stifling heat forced Pablo to open his door. People walking by saw a short and stocky male dressed in only a loincloth standing in front of his easel.

As the seasons changed, Pablo's gloomy mood, which was reflected in his paintings, remained the same until one fateful day. On the afternoon of August 4, 1904, a woman by the name of Fernande Olivier came into his life. The chance encounter blossomed into a long-term relationship. Both of them were happy. Gradually, the color of rose replaced the once-gloomy blue. Circus performers and clowns now took center stage on his new canvases. His luck was changing.

One day, an art dealer who once rejected Pablo's work decided to buy thirty paintings for two thousand francs. That was enough to live off for three years! A few years later, a Russian art collector bought fifty of Pablo's paintings at one time. From then on, Pablo never had to worry about money again.

Pablo is considered to be the greatest artist of the twentieth century.
Who was he?

PABLO PICASSO

Pablo Picasso had a great deal of talent, but it was always his willingness to practice and perfect his talent that brought him wealth and fame.

PABLO PICASSO'S BIO

Birth Name: Pablo Diego Jose Francisco de Paula Juan
               Nepomuceno Maria de los Remedios Cipriano de la
               Santisima Trinidad Martyr Patricio Clito Ruiz y
               Picasso

               (He was baptized with this long name in honor of
               various saints and relatives. Ruiz is the surname for his
               mother and Picasso is the surname for his father.)

Birthplace: Malaga, Spain
Birth Date: October 25, 1881
Died: April 8, 1973
Age: Ninety-one years old

ACHIEVEMENTS

Picasso developed a new artistic movement called Cubism (1909–1912)
with Georges Braque. This style of painting used monochrome brownish
and neutral colors. Both artists took apart objects and "analyzed" them
in terms of their shapes.

Picasso was amazingly productive throughout his life. It has been
estimated that he produced fifty thousand pieces of artwork, which
consisted of paintings, sculptures, ceramics, drawings, prints, tapestries,
and rugs.

Selected Quotes by Pablo Picasso

"I am always doing that which I cannot do, in order that I may learn how to do it."

"Others have seen what is and asked why. I have seen what could be and asked why not."

"Inspiration does exist, but it must find you working."

"I do not seek. I find."

"Every child is an artist. The problem is how to remain an artist once he grows up."

"Everything you can imagine is real."

"I paint objects as I think them, not as I see them."

"I begin with an idea and then it becomes something else."

"The artist is a receptacle for the emotions that come from all over the place: from the sky, from the earth, from a scrap of paper, from a passing shape, from a spider's web."

"There are painters who transform the sun to a yellow spot, but there are others who with the help of their art and their intelligence, transform a yellow spot into the sun."

"There is no abstract art. You must always start with something. Afterward you can remove all traces of reality."

"Give me a museum and I'll fill it."

"Good taste is the enemy of creativity."

"Art is the elimination of the unnecessary."

"Painting is just another way of keeping a diary."

"Art washes away from the soul the dust of everyday life."

"What I don't like is that just because one painter has been successful in some style they all have to follow in his tracks. I don't believe in following any particular school, for all it leads to is mannerism and affectation in the painters who do it."

"Our goals can only be reached through a vehicle of a plan, in which we must fervently believe, and upon which we must vigorously act. There is no other route to success. To draw you must close your eyes and sing."

"He can who thinks he can, and he can't who thinks he can't. This is an inexorable, indisputable law."

FURTHER READING

Picasso: Creator and Destroyer by Arianna Stassinopoulos
Portrait of Picasso as a Young Man by Norman Mailer
A Life of Picasso: The Prodigy, 1881–1906 by John Richardson

NEVER STOP LEARNING

Little Marian always followed her father to church. Her favorite thing to do was to hum along with the choir. So, Dad enrolled his six-year-old in the junior choir. Shortly thereafter, Marian was given a part in a duet. Four years later, she was promoted to the senior choir and sang her first solo. As she sang, Dad sat proudly as he watched his daughter's debut.

Unfortunately, Dad's fate did not allow him to hear his daughter sing for long. By the time Marian was thirteen, Dad died as a result of an accident at work where an object fell on his head. Life was never the same after Christmas 1910 in Philadelphia.

Without the breadwinner, Marian, with her mother and two younger sisters, moved into her grandparents' tiny house. Mom found some menial jobs and opened a home laundry service to wash and iron other people's clothes. The girls helped by arranging for pick-up and delivery and collecting money. Besides helping out her mother, Marian had school during the day and choir practice at night.

Marian was a natural contralto, one who sings comfortably in the lowest female range. But her voice had the rare ability to go from the low level of a baritone all the way up to that of a soprano. Because of her unique talent, she was called on to substitute for various soloists on a number of occasions.

One day, Marian was invited to perform at a gala concert where she would share the stage with the famous Negro tenor, Roland Hayes. After the concert, Mr. Hayes paid a visit to Marian's home. "She has a great gift, and she ought to have a teacher,"[1] he said. He went on to suggest that Marian could study under his former voice teacher in Boston for free. But Grandmother disapproved. "No girl her age has any business living anywhere except in her own home!"[2] said her grandmother. Old-fashioned Grandma had just dashed Marian's hopes.

But Mom was more supportive. "Don't grieve over it, baby," Mom said, "If it's the right thing for you, a way will be opened. You just go on doing the best you can in school, and we'll see."[3]

Mom was right. Not long after, a friend introduced Marian to Mary Saunders Patterson, who was a voice teacher. After listening to Marian sing, she offered to give her free lessons, which Marian gladly accepted. Six months later, she had learned all that Mary could teach her. "If you are going on with your music, you really ought to learn more than I can teach you. You ought to go to a music school,"[4] Mary recommended. Marian heeded her advice and made her way to the conservatory nearby.

"I would like a registration form,"[5] Marian requested. "We don't take colored,"[6] the girl announced. Then she slammed the window in the registrar's office. Shocked and confused, Marian returned home to her mother, who repeated the encouraging words she gave before.

During her final year in high school, she met Giuseppe Boghetti, a highly regarded vocal coach. Her principal, Dr. Lucy Wilson, arranged the meeting with the help of one of Mr. Boghetti's pupils, Lisa Roma. "I have more pupils than I need already. I listen to you only as a favor to Miss Roma. Understand?"[7] Mr. Boghetti uttered.

After Marian finished her piece, Mr. Boghetti was impressed. "I will teach you," he said. "You will study with me two years. At the end of that time, you will be able to sing anywhere!"[8]

There was one problem. Marian couldn't afford the lessons. When the church leaders heard about this, they organized a concert and raised over six hundred dollars for Marian.

Mr. Boghetti was just the teacher Marian needed. "Nature has given you a voice," the Italian coach instructed Marian, "but there is no shortcut to becoming a real professional. Only when you understand the *how* and *why* of singing will you be able to perform well no matter how you feel."[9] She didn't disappoint Mr. Boghetti. Over time, Marian evened out her tones for a smoother sound, improved her breathing for more volume, and added new arias to her ever-increasing repertoire.

In between lessons, Marian teamed up with Billy King as her piano player and performed in a number of different places, from churches and theaters to clubs and private homes. Gradually, her celebrity status grew, and so did her income. By the time Marian was twenty, she was making enough money to realize one of her dreams—to buy her mother a house.

One day, a concert promoter approached Marian with the idea of performing at Town Hall in New York City. She had never performed on such a big stage as Town Hall, but she felt ready for her big debut. But she wasn't. After the concert, a critic pointed out her flaw: "She sang her Brahms as if by rote."[10] She didn't understand German and here she was singing German songs without knowing the words, only the sounds associated with them.

This was a fatal blow to her once-promising career. Afterward, she quit singing. No words from Mom could lift her spirits. For a year, she avoided Billy and Mr. Boghetti. Then one day, her mother was put under doctor's order to rest. And yet, she got up early the next day for work. Marian ordered her mother back to bed and picked up the phone. "I want to tell you my mother won't be coming in today," she told the supervisor. "Not today or ever again."[11] Then Marian quickly made a second call. "Billy? This is Marian. I'm ready to go back to work."[12]

To rebuild her confidence, Mr. Boghetti suggested that Marian enter a local singing contest. She won. Then she entered another. Again, she was victorious. This time she beat out three hundred contestants who came from all over the country and won an appearance with the New York Philharmonic Orchestra. Her performance in New York brought good reviews this time. Requests came pouring in. Right away, a concert promoter offered her a contract. But after two years, she was appearing in the same venues with the same pay.

Frustrated by lack of progress, Marian decided to get additional training. So, she went to Europe to study with the best teachers she could find. First, she went to England. A year later, she headed off to Berlin to learn German so that she could add more meaning and feelings to her Brahms. Her hard work was beginning to pay off. At the end of her lesson one day, two gentlemen approached her with an offer to tour Europe.

With Rule Rasmussen as the manager and Kosti Vehanen as the pianist, the three of them embarked on a six-month tour of Scandinavia. It was a huge success. "That first trip to the Scandinavian countries was an encouragement and incentive. It made me realize that the time and energy invested in seeking to become an artist were worthwhile, and that what I had dared to aspire to was not impossible,"[13] Marian said.

She went back to Europe for a few more tours. Everywhere she went, she received immense acclaim and rave reviews. Marian's growing fame finally caught the attention of Sol Hurok, a top concert promoter in America. A contract was offered and signed. Marian returned to the United States with Kosti as her accompanist by her side.

Back home, Marian enchanted her audiences just like she had in Europe. One day, Sol decided to book Constitution Hall in Washington, DC, but the owners, a society called the Daughters of the American Revolution, turned him down when they discovered that Marian was black. First Lady Eleanor Roosevelt was so outraged by the fact that she immediately resigned her membership. She then proceeded to help arrange a free outdoor concert in front of the Lincoln Memorial. On April 9, 1939, with sunny skies, Marian stood in front of seventy-five thousand people of all colors and let her beautiful voice soar.

Richard Lam

During her professional singing career, she was considered the world's greatest contralto. Who was she?

MARIAN ANDERSON

Marian Anderson had a remarkably long career that lasted into her sixties. Her talent alone did not make her world famous. It was her commitment to constantly learn and practice that did.

MARIAN ANDERSON'S BIO

Birth Name:	Marian Anderson
Birthplace:	Philadelphia, Pennsylvania, United States
Birth Date:	February 27, 1897
Died:	April 8, 1993
Age:	Ninety-six years old

ACHIEVEMENTS

During her career, she toured in Scandinavia, Europe, South America, Jamaica and the West Indies, Japan and the Far East, Israel, Morocco, Tunisia, and Canada.

In the United States alone, she performed in more than six hundred cities.

On January 7, 1955, Anderson became the first African American to perform with the New York Metropolitan Opera.

SELECTED QUOTES BY MARIAN ANDERSON

"When I sing, I don't want them to see that my face is black. I don't want them to see that my face is white. I want them to see my soul. And that is colorless."

"None of us is responsible for the complexion of his skin. This fact of nature offers no clue to the character or quality of the person underneath."

"The Negro or the white person must be judged as an individual, with all his goodness or badness, and the color of his skin makes no difference. He who made us all did not make any mistake when he made us of a different color."

"When you stop having dreams and ideals, well, you might as well stop altogether."

"I suppose I might insist on making issues of things. But that is not my nature, and I always bear in mind that my mission is to leave behind me the kind of impression that will make it easier for those who follow."

"Fear is a disease that eats away at logic and makes man inhuman."

"Leadership should be born out of the understanding of the needs of those who would be affected by it."

"The minute a person whose word means a great deal to others dare to take the open-hearted and courageous way, many others follow."

"Everyone has a gift for something, even if it is the gift of being a good friend."

"There are many persons ready to do what is right because in their hearts they know it is right. But they hesitate, waiting for the other fellow to make the make the first move—and he, in turn, waits for you."

"No matter how big a nation is, it is no stronger that its weakest people, and as long as you keep a person down, some part of you has to be down there to hold him down, so it means you cannot soar as you might otherwise."

"You lose a lot of time, hating people."

FURTHER READING

My Lord, What a Morning: An Autobiography by Marian Anderson
Marian Anderson: Singing to the World by Janet Stevenson
Marian Anderson: Lady from Philadelphia by Shirlee P. Newman

Golden Opportunities

Albert was a daydreamer. Growing up, he was only a mediocre student. Books bored him. He spent most of his time just thinking about things. "I'd imagine all kinds of situations and how I would handle them,"[1] he said. Oftentimes his mother wondered about him. "What are you doing, Albert?"[2] his mother would ask. "Nothing, just thinking,"[3] he replied. "Daydreaming you mean?"[4] she teased.

Thanks to Mom, the nickname Danny Dreamer eventually caught on and remained popular even when he was in high school. But he wasn't just a dreamer. When he dreamt about having a lemonade stand, it wasn't long before he was selling the sweet and sour refreshment. "I never considered my dreams wasted energy; they were invariably linked to some form of action,"[5] he said.

By the time he was fifteen, he decided to see the world. So, he volunteered as an ambulance driver for the Red Cross. Although he was too young for the training program, he lied about his age to get accepted. However, he was never deployed to France because the First World War had just ended. So, Albert returned home to Chicago, not knowing what to do next.

By now, school was out of the question. Instead, he decided to use his sales skills and musical talent to make a living. During the day, he sold ribbon novelties to women who enjoyed sewing and doing arts and crafts. At night, he played the piano for a local radio station and at clubs around town. Soon, he was making more money than his father.

When Albert got married in 1922, he had begun to work full-time for the Lily Tulip Company selling paper cups. For the next sixteen years, he was able to provide a comfortable living for his wife and daughter. Then one day, he ran into Earl Prince, the inventor of the five-spindled "Multimixer" milkshake machine, which can make five milkshakes simultaneously. He was amazed by what the mixer could do. Sensing a strong demand for this new invention, Albert seized the opportunity and signed an exclusive deal with Earl to be the distributor. For the first time in his life, Albert was his own boss. The more milkshake machines he sold, the more money he made.

This new business venture had lots of potential, but it was very risky. Albert had to mortgage his home and invest his entire life savings to get the rights to sell Multimixers exclusively. "You are risking your whole future if you do this, Albert,"[6] his wife warned. "You just have to trust my instincts. I am positive this is going to be a winner,"[7] he assured her.

With the Multimixer in hand, he traveled all over the country peddling the milkshake machine to owners of ice cream parlors and restaurants. For ten years, the Multimixer business was very profitable. By the late 1940s, he was making twenty-five thousand dollars a year, which was a great deal of money at the time. But soon after, sales of the Multimixer plummeted due to competition from other mixer manufacturers and a new, popular dessert, soft-served ice cream.

He began to brainstorm to save his business. Ordinarily, most ice cream parlors and restaurants bought one or maybe two Multimixers. So when he heard that a small fast-food drive-in was running eight Multimixers, making forty milkshakes simultaneously, he just had to see it to believe it. In 1954, he headed west to San Bernardino, California, to check out this little hamburger stand.

He had never seen anything like it. This place had a simple menu that included fifteen-cent hamburgers, French fries, and milkshakes. Customers were being served so quickly that the place resembled an assembly line. What was amazing was the customers never stopped coming. At least 150 customers showed up during lunch and dinner time.

The two brothers, Richard and Maurice McDonald, who opened their restaurant in 1940, ran an extremely efficient operation that was very profitable. Right away, Albert's imagination took hold. He felt that the fast-food industry was about to take off and a drive-in like the McDonald's would be successful in cities all over the United States. More importantly, each new McDonald's that opened would mean that he could sell at least eight more Multimixers. So, here was a golden opportunity he couldn't let go.

He returned home excited by the prospect of huge Multimixer sales. "I was fifty-two years old. I had diabetes and incipient arthritis. I had lost my gall bladder and most of my thyroid gland, but I was convinced that the best was ahead of me,"[8] he said. Coincidentally, the McDonald brothers were looking for a new agent to turn their hamburger stand into a franchise. They wanted to open more hamburger stands like theirs using their name.

After pondering for a week, Albert came up with a radical idea. Instead of just selling Multimixers to the brothers, why not become their franchising agent, too? Albert's sales pitch worked, as usual. Richard and Maurice agreed to give him the exclusive rights to franchise their drive-in nationwide. This was 1953.

Albert opened his own McDonald's in Des Plaines, Illinois, on April 15, 1955, putting in seventy hours a week. His McDonald's, which was built identically to the original drive-in, would serve as a model for potential investors. But success didn't come easy, and many challenges lay ahead. First, Albert had to find investors who were interested in opening a McDonald's. Then, he learned that some of the new owners or franchisees didn't follow the McDonald's system. Some franchisees charged different prices, while others offered different items on their menu. This was not going to work. Albert knew that this lack of uniformity would soon destroy his McDonald's Corporation. So, he proposed a standard operating procedure that was based on quality, cleanliness, service, and value. Every McDonald's operator would adhere to this new set of strict guidelines.

Another big challenge was perfecting the French fries. For a while, Albert just couldn't reproduce the same great taste in the French fries as the McDonald's brothers, even when he followed their procedure exactly. Finally, the problem was solved when he learned that the potatoes first had to be cured for three weeks in a dry environment. Yet, he wasn't satisfied. Over the next ten years, his company spent three million dollars to come up with the best-tasting fries in the industry.

Under Albert's strong leadership, more and more McDonald's restaurants opened up across the country. When his employees and franchisees came up with new ideas, Albert gave them the freedom to test their creativity. Soon, new products such as the Filet-O-Fish and the Big Mac were introduced to stay ahead of the competition. His franchisees were the first to place restaurant advertisements on local radio and television. In less than ten years, McDonald's became the leader in the fast-food industry. For all of his hard work, Albert's big payday finally came. On April 15, 1965, the McDonald's Corporation went public. Within a few weeks, the stock price soared. Albert's share of stock was worth thirty-two million dollars.

Today, there are more than thirty-one thousand McDonald's restaurants in the United States and around the globe. Who was the founder of McDonald's?

Ray Kroc

Ray Kroc never stopped working for McDonald's. He worked into his late seventies. He seized his opportunities and always worked hard to turn those opportunities into success.

Ray Kroc's Bio

Birth Name: Ray Albert Kroc
Birthplace: Chicago, Illinois, United States
Birth Date: October 5, 1902
Died: January 14, 1984
Age: Eighty-one years old

Achievements

1961:   Founded Hamburger University as a training center emphasizing quality service

1963:   Ronald McDonald makes first TV appearance

1965:   The Filet-O-Fish appears on the menu

1968:   The Big Mac appears on the menu

1973:   The Egg McMuffin and Quarter Pounder appear on the menu

1974:   Established Ronald McDonald House to help families of critically ill children

1979:   The Happy Meal appears on the menu

Richard Lam

Selected Quotes by Ray Kroc

"A man must take advantage of any opportunity that comes along."

"Achievement must be made against the possibility of failure, the risk of defeat. Where there is no risk, there can be no pride in achievement and consequently, no happiness. The only way we can advance is by going forward, individually and collectively, in the spirit of the pioneer."

"If you think small you'll stay small."

"I have always believed that each man makes his own happiness and is responsible for his own problems."

"Work is the meat in the hamburger of life."

"Luck is a dividend of sweat. The more you sweat, the luckier you get."

"The key to closing a sale is to know when to stop selling."

"Too many salesmen, I found, would make a good presentation and convince the client, but they couldn't recognize that critical moment when they should have stopped talking."

"If someone only likes making money, I'm not attracted to them. I like anybody who likes what he's doing, because that's the thing that I treasure most."

"If you've got time to lean, you've got time to clean."

"As long as you're green you're growing, as soon as you're ripe you start to rot."

"The quality of a leader is reflected in the standards he sets for himself."

FURTHER READING

Grinding It Out: The Making of McDonald's by Ray Kroc
McDonald's: Behind the Arches by John F. Love

No Matter What They Say

She had just won a poetry recital contest at school. "You were lucky, Hilda,"[1] the deputy headmistress sneered. "I was not lucky," Hilda roared. "I deserved it."[2] At only nine years of age, Hilda already possessed a great deal of self-confidence.

Education was strongly emphasized at home. "Homework always had to be completed—even if that meant doing it on Sunday evening,"[3] Hilda recalled. After homework was completed, she and her older sister went downstairs to the family-owned grocery store to help out her parents. "One of the tasks I sometimes shared was the weighing out of tea, sugar, and biscuits from the sacks and boxes in which they arrived into one and two-pound bags,"[4] she remembered. On Saturdays, Hilda helped her father make deliveries and take orders as they roamed the neighborhood.

When the girls weren't working, Dad made sure that they took advantage of every educational opportunity. He took them along to seminars on current and international affairs at the local university. Of the two sisters, it was Hilda who shared her father's attitude and interests in learning. After graduating from primary school, she attended Kesteven and Grantham Girls' School in England, where she excelled. Except for her last year, she finished first in her class every year. She didn't play many sports, although she did learn to swim and joined the school field hockey team.

At home, she played the usual board games like Monopoly and Pit. However, by 1939, all fun and games practically came to an end once Great Britain entered World War II. Hilda was almost fourteen when the war broke out. Soon after, Germany began dropping bombs on her hometown in Grantham. Altogether, there were twenty-one bombings, which resulted in seventy-eight deaths. "During air raids we would crawl under the table for shelter—we had no outside shelter for we had no garden—until the 'all clear' sounded,"[5] Hilda recalled.

These were about the only times when Hilda and Dad had to put their books down. Every week, he borrowed a "serious" book for the two of them and a novel for Mom. Hilda was reading books that girls of her age normally didn't read. "I soon knew what I liked—anything about politics and international affairs,"[6] Hilda said. But when she applied for college, she decided to major in science instead. There were a couple of reasons for this. She did well in math and science and knew that people with science skills were in high demand, especially in wartime Britain. And because fewer women studied science in college this meant she had a better chance of being accepted at a top university.

However, her top choice, Somerville College, one of Oxford's oldest women's colleges, put her on the waiting list. This was a bitter disappointment for the seventeen-year-old hopeful. Then, suddenly, a telegram arrived. By luck, a last-minute cancellation opened a spot for her. Wasting no time, she quickly packed her bags and headed off to Oxford. There, she concentrated on studying chemistry. "I threw myself into intensely hard work,"[7] Hilda said.

Soon, her political interests led her to join the Oxford University Conservative Association (OUCA) where she received lessons in public speaking and learned to answer questions in front of a critical audience. Her hard work and devotion to the OUCA quickly gained the respect of her fellow members, most of which were men.

In October 1946, Hilda was elected president of OUCA. She was devoting so much time to the OUCA that her studies began to suffer. By the time Hilda graduated with a second-class degree in chemistry, she had found her calling: public service. She wanted to study law. But first she needed a job to pay the bills. So with her chemistry degree in hand, she landed a job as a research chemist with the British Xylonite Plastics Company. During this time, Hilda joined the local political organization called the Conservative Association.

Not long after, in January 1949, a friend told her that the Conservative Association in Dartford was looking for candidates to run for the seat for Member of Parliament representing Dartford. She submitted her application immediately. "I had told the selection committee that I would fight for Dartford with all the energy at my disposal, and I meant it,"[8] Hilda said. She worked extremely hard for the right to represent as the conservative candidate for the town of Dartford. "The 1950 election campaign was the most exhausting few weeks I had ever spent,"[9] she said.

The selection committee was so impressed by her level of energy and dedication that they selected her over twenty-six other male applicants. In February 1949, Hilda became the youngest parliamentary candidate in Britain. But she lost the general election in 1950 and again in 1951. However, each time she came away with valuable lessons.

After a short time, any ill feelings caused by the defeats were replaced with joy. In December 1951, Hilda married Denis, a wealthy businessman whom she met two years earlier while doing work for the Conservative Party. "Now with Denis's support I could afford to concentrate on legal studies without taking up new employment,"[10] Hilda said. Two and half years later, in May 1953, five months pregnant, Hilda passed the first bar exam. By August, she had delivered fraternal twins, seven weeks prematurely.

In December that year, she passed her bar final exam, which led to an apprenticeship at a tax law firm. But after a six-month tryout, the law firm didn't hire her. Unhappy but undeterred, she quickly found a new position as a full-time tax barrister. Over the next five years, she thought constantly about one thing: getting back into politics.

With the twins only a year old, she jumped back into the political arena. She applied to the selection committees all over London and the surrounding areas. Each one turned her down. They were impressed by her qualifications and intelligence but they questioned her ability to perform public service as a young mother of two babies. "I was hurt and disappointed by these experiences. But I refused to be put off by them. I was confident that I had something to offer in politics,"[11] Hilda said.

Finally, after four years of rejections, the selection committee at Finchley, located due north of London, picked her over one hundred fifty applicants. She seized the opportunity by pouring all her energy into the campaign. Every day from 8 AM until after dark, Hilda reached out to her constituents in this five-and-half-square-mile town and pledged for their support by visiting shops, senior citizen homes, offices, schools, and even union halls. She was always well-prepared. "I prepared my speech until it was word perfect, and I had mastered the technique of talking without notes,"[12] Hilda said.

Her hard work finally paid off. In 1959, this thirty-four-year-old woman defeated two male opponents to become the youngest Member of Parliament in the House of Commons. Because of her work ethic and intelligence, the prime minister promoted her to a position in the ministry of pensions and national insurance after only two years of service. More promotions followed. With each new post, Hilda learned more about the inner workings of government. She was steadily gaining the respect and support of her Conservative Party.

However, the opposing Labor Party saw her as a major threat. While serving as secretary of state for education and science in 1970, she came under attack. They called her the "Milk Snatcher" for taking away free milk from schoolchildren in an effort to reduce government spending. Night after night, she came home exhausted by the constant criticism and pressure. "The criticism was vicious," she said later. "You have to build armor around yourself to cope."[13] Sometimes Hilda cracked under the immense pressure and cried.

One night, Denis tried to convince her to quit. "Why don't you chuck it all in? You don't have to put up with this. Why go on?"[14] Hilda looked up with tears running down her cheeks. "I'll see them in hell first," she fired back. "I will never be driven anywhere against my will!"[15]

In 1979, Hilda became the first female prime minister of Great
Britain. Who was this tenacious leader?

Margaret Thatcher

Margaret Thatcher never let any obstacles get in her way. She always had the self-confidence and the belief to succeed no matter what people said.

MARGARET THATCHER'S BIO

Birth Name: Margaret Hilda Roberts
Birthplace: Grantham, Lincolnshire, England
Birth Date: October 13, 1925
Died:
Age: Eighty-three years old

ACHIEVEMENTS

Served as Member of Parliament for Finchley from October 8, 1959 to April 9, 1992

Served as secretary of state for education and science from June 20, 1970 to March 4, 1974

Served as prime minister of the United Kingdom from May 4, 1979 to November 28, 1990

Selected Quotes by Margaret Thatcher

"Defeat—I do not recognize the meaning of the word!"

"I fight on, I fight to win."

"I do not know anyone who has got to the top without hard work. That is the recipe. It will not always get you to the top, but should get you pretty near."

"People think that at the top there isn't much room. They tend to think of it as an Everest. My message is that there is tons of room at the top."

"What is success? I think it is a mixture of having a flair for the thing that you are doing; knowing that it is not enough, that you have got to have hard work and a certain sense of purpose."

"You may have to fight a battle more than once to win it."

"I've got a woman's ability to stick to a job and get on with it when everyone else walks off and leaves it."

"I always cheer up immensely if an attack is particularly wounding because I think, well, if they attack one personally, it means they have not a single political argument left."

"I'm extraordinarily patient provided I get my own way in the end."

"I am in politics because of the conflict between good and evil, and I believe that in the end good will triumph."

"It pays to know the enemy—not least because at some time you may have the opportunity to turn him into a friend."

"Look at a day when you are supremely satisfied at the end. It's not a day when you lounge around doing nothing; it's when you've had everything to do and you've done it."

"Disciplining yourself to do what you know is right and important, although difficult, is the high road to pride, self-esteem, and personal satisfaction."

"Plan your work for today and every day, then work your plan."

FURTHER READING

Margaret Thatcher: The Path to Power by Margaret Thatcher
Margaret Thatcher: The Woman Within by Andrew Thomson
Maggie: An Intimate Portrait of a Woman in Power by Chris Ogden

CLIMB AS HIGH AS YOU CAN

As a kid, Percival was physically below average. "I was generally smaller and weaker than most of my fellow pupils and never became fully involved in school sports or other activities,"[1] he said. Even if Percival wanted to participate, Mom didn't allow any fun and games. She was afraid that he might hang out with the wrong crowd. So instead of playing games, Percival received a great deal of beneficial instruction from his mother.

"Mother was a woman of admirable character and gave me the affection and encouragement I needed,"[2] he said. On the other hand, Dad's strict standards did not always agree with his rebellious young son. All through his teenage years, Percival got into heated arguments that quite often resulted in disciplinary action. "My father believed in the necessity of corporal punishment, and we had many memorable confrontations in the wood shed,"[3] he remembered.

To escape from his parental pressures, Percival often wandered into his imaginary world and conjured up wild dreams and fantasies in which he always played the hero. But whatever confidence he had about his physical appearance, it was soon shattered by his high school gym teacher. "He placed me in the misfit class with the other physical freaks and devoted his main attention to the more adequately equipped schoolboys. I developed a feeling of inferiority about my physique which has remained with me to this day—it wasn't an inferiority about what I could achieve, but a solid conviction about how appalling I looked,"[4] he said. In his spare time, Percival devoured books at a rate of one per day over a period of time. His favorites always had something to do with adventure.

Up to now, Percival was still considered to be a puny little kid. Then, to everyone's surprise, his scrawny physique underwent a rapid transformation. He grew five inches one year and four inches the next.

His lean muscles got stronger. By the time he graduated from high school, before reaching sixteen, he was doing a man's work at the family honey business, which owned sixteen hundred beehives. During harvest season, Percival handled thousands of ninety-pound boxes of honeycomb for extraction and endured his daily dosage of a dozen or more beestings. In the summer, the family worked every day of the week from dawn till dusk, frequently late into the night. "I'd worked hard for some years in the business without receiving any pay—not even pocket money,"[5] Percival recalled.

He had to beg his father for money so that he could go on a ten-day vacation with a friend. For two years, he went to college but then dropped out to work full-time for his father. When his country, New Zealand, declared war on the Japanese, Percival immediately applied to join the air force to be a pilot. For the longest time, flying offered everything that he wanted: adventure, independence, and freedom. Shortly thereafter, he withdrew his application because his conscience told him that it was wrong to kill. So the beekeeper begrudgingly buzzed back to the beehives. "I was very restless and unhappy and the first few years of the war were the most uncertain and miserable of my life,"[6] Percival recalled. He was working very hard, but as usual, Percival had little time for entertainment.

By summer 1940, the twenty-year-old desperately needed a break. So he convinced his dad to let him go on a short trip with a friend to a famous resort called the Hermitage in the Southern Alps of New Zealand. There, sitting in the lounge that first evening, Percival overheard something that piqued his interest. Whispers swirled the room about the two men who just walked in. The word was these adventurers had just climbed Mount Cook, the highest mountain in New Zealand. Listening quietly in a corner, the young beekeeper was overcome with envy. "Tomorrow I must climb something!"[7] Percival proclaimed.

Following the footsteps of their guide, Percival and his companion reached the summit of Mount Oliver, a small peak above the Hermitage. The feeling of freedom and exhilaration gained by climbing to the top was the happiest moment of his life. As time passed, Percival's thoughts once again turned to the air force. By now, his school friends were in the service, and his enthusiasm for adventure was too great to be challenged. At the beginning of 1944, his life of adventure took off when the Royal New Zealand Air Force called.

Between military trainings, Percival pursued his new passion. Week after week, Percival went climbing either by himself or with a friend and conquered one peak after another. By Christmas 1944, he felt ready to climb Mount Cook. But when he got a closer view of it and saw its large faces covered with thick ice, he retreated with cold feet. "I'd built up quite a lot of confidence over the previous year but now I realized how little I really knew,"[8] Percival admitted. He wasn't aware of life-threatening dangers, such as deep crevices and avalanches.

After a serious boating accident, Percival was discharged from military duty and returned home to recuperate from his burns. Thereafter, he resumed his beekeeping duties and favorite pastime. Up until now, Percival had learned mountain climbing techniques only through books and alpine journals. He had no instructor until he met Harry Ayres, one of New Zealand's legendary climbers. Harry taught Percival a great deal about safe yet aggressive mountaineering. One day in the summer of 1947, the two went out and reached the apex of Mount Cook at 12,329 feet. "Many of my best days were spent with Harry Ayres, and many of my best climbs done under the umbrella of his skill,"[9] Percival said.

From that point on, Percival gained the confidence and courage to climb higher and higher. In the summer of 1950, he went on a climbing trip to Switzerland and conquered Jungfrau at 13,642 feet. By then, his reputation as a mountaineer was growing. One day, a group of New Zealand mountaineers invited Percival to join them on an expedition to the Himalayas. Percival gladly accepted the invitation. The team reached an elevation of 22,180 feet before retreating from adverse weather conditions. When Percival reached the bottom of the Himalayas, there was a telegram inviting him to join the British expedition to explore the possibilities of conquering Mount Everest.

No one had ever set foot on top of the world's highest mountain at 29,028 feet. Some of the world's best climbers died trying. Falls, extreme cold, lack of oxygen, or exhaustion were the main causes. The following year, in 1952, Percival rejoined the British expedition to attempt Cho Oyu at 26,870 feet as a test run prior to attempting Everest. But they failed. Nonetheless, the team learned a great deal from the experience. A year later, the British expedition blitzed Everest with over four hundred people, including three hundred sixty-two porters and twenty Sherpa guides who helped carry food, supplies, and equipment up the dangerous slopes. After nearly two months of overcoming subzero temperatures, blustery winds, and numerous dangerous obstacles, Percival and his Sherpa friend, Tenzing Norgay, made the final ascent to the top of the world at 11:30 AM on May 29, 1953.

Richard Lam

Percival became an instant hero. Who was this courageous
mountaineer?

EDMUND HILLARY

For fifteen minutes, Edmund Hillary stood on top of the world. It was always his courage, hard work, and determination that took him to the peak of the world's highest mountains.

EDMUND HILLARY'S BIO

Birth Name:	Edmund Percival Hillary
Birthplace:	Auckland, New Zealand
Birth Date:	July 20, 1919
Died:	January 11, 2008
Age:	Eighty-eight years old

ACHIEVEMENTS

First person to reach the summit of Mount Everest

After conquering Mount Everest, he devoted much of his life to helping the Sherpa people of Nepal through the Himalayan Trust, a charity organization he founded. Many schools and hospitals were built.

SELECTED QUOTES BY EDMUND HILLARY

"Someday I'm going to climb Everest."

"The mediocre can have adventures and even the fearful can achieve."

"You don't have to be a fantastic hero to do certain things—to compete. You can be just an ordinary chap, sufficiently motivated."

"It is not the mountain we conquer but ourselves."

"In some ways I believe I epitomize the average New Zealander: I have modest abilities, I combine these with a good deal of determination, and I rather like to succeed."

"Each of us has to discover his own path. Some paths will be spectacular and others peaceful and quiet—who is to say which is the most important? For me the most rewarding moments have not always been the great moments—for what can surpass a tear on your departure, joy on your return, or a trusting hand in yours?"

"I was never one to obsess about the past. Too much to do in the future!"

FURTHER READING

Nothing Venture, Nothing Win by Edmund Hillary
View from the Summit by Edmund Hillary
Reaching the Summit: Sir Edmund Hillary's Life of Adventure by Alexa Johnston

Always Be Curious

Grief came too soon for Manya. By the age of ten, her mother had succumbed to tuberculosis, and her oldest sister had died from typhus two years earlier. These two unforgettable losses drove the youngest child in the family into a state of depression and isolation. For hours or sometimes days at a time, Manya escaped from her cruel world to seek comfort by reading books. School became a sanctuary in which she excelled.

By summer 1883, she had graduated high school first in her class with a gold medal just like her older siblings, sister Bronya and brother Joseph. After enduring years of misery and pressure to perform well in school, the health of this fifteen-year-old finally broke down. Manya kept to her room without any appetite for food. Worried, Dad sent Manya to live with relatives in the countryside where she could recuperate in the quiet fresh air. A year later, the happy and rejuvenated Manya returned home only to face the same financial struggles as before.

The meager pay from Dad's job as a secondary-school teacher could barely pay for food and rent. So Manya and Bronya took charge to help out the family by tutoring at the lowly rate of half a ruble per hour. But Manya quickly changed her mind. The income was not worth the effort of walking long distances across town in the rain and cold to teach lazy students whose parents sometimes forgot to pay. She resigned and went to work as a governess for a wealthy family instead. But after three months, she had had enough of the snobbish family, who exploited their servants.

Manya's heart ached. Deep inside, this compassionate young woman felt responsible for the family's future. She also knew that Bronya had been yearning to go to the University of Paris in France to study medicine. But there was no money to send her abroad. One day, Manya approached her sister with a plan. It was indeed possible to send Bronya to Paris with the financial aid from Manya and Dad.

"To start with, you will spend your own money. After that I'll arrange to send you some; Father, too. And at the same time I'll be piling up money for my own future studies. When you are a doctor it will be my turn to go. And then you will help me,"[1] she advised Bronya.

Tears welled from her sister's eyes.

"I don't understand. You don't hope to make enough money for your own support and part of mine and then still more to save, do you?"[2] Bronya inquired.

"I am going to get a job as governess in a family. With board, lodging, and laundry all free, I shall have four hundred rubles a year in wages, perhaps more,"[3] Manya assured her.

With an excellent academic record and fluency in five languages, Manya had little trouble landing a job as the governess for the Zorawski family. She knew very well that this job would mean isolation from her family for a number of years. Yet, the eighteen-year-old made the sacrifice to help her family.

Once her daily chores of giving lessons to the two Zorawski children were finished, Manya turned to advancing her own education at night. Gradually, she became more and more interested in mathematics and physics. "The method was not efficacious, but I acquired the habit of independent work and I learned a certain number of things which were to be useful to me later,"[4] Manya recalled. As promised, she sent her sister funds—fifteen rubles every month and sometimes twenty— nearly half her salary.

After nearly eight years of hard work and sacrifice, Manya finally realized her own dream of attending the famous University of Paris, at the age of twenty-four. When she got to Paris, she quickly discovered that her self-taught mathematics and physics coursework was deficient. She studied nonstop to catch up. Nothing mattered more, not even her tough living conditions. She rented a tiny attic with a small skylight for twenty francs a month. There was no heat, electricity, or water, just some light that came through the little square window. To save money, Manya walked to the university in all types of weather. The poor girl would stay at the library of Sainte-Genevieve until the doors closed at ten o'clock. Then she returned to the attic and burned the midnight oil until two in the morning before she rested her eyes. Her daily diet primarily consisted of buttered bread and tea. Occasionally, she indulged on some eggs, a piece of chocolate, or some fruit.

By July 1894, after three years of hard work, Manya passed her master's examination in mathematics and physics with high marks. Having accomplished her mission, she reluctantly returned to her homeland to rejoin her father even though she really wanted to stay at the university for more advanced study. She loved the free atmosphere of conducting experiments in the laboratory very much. But once again poverty got in the way of her dream. She had no more money for further education.

Soon after, fortune came her way. A Samaritan by the name of Ms. Dydynska secured a scholarship for Manya to return to Paris. The prize of six hundred rubles was enough to live on for fifteen months. Upon her return, her professor, Gabriel Lippmann, offered Manya six hundred francs to determine the magnetic properties of various steels. But the work proved very challenging. So she sought help from a male physicist who was an expert on the laws of magnetism. Manya knew that Pierre had invented a number of scientific instruments that might help with her work. The two scientists quickly developed a productive working relationship. Right away, Pierre was smitten by Manya's intelligence, work ethic, and courage. The following year, on July 26, 1895, they were married in a simple ceremony in the garden of Pierre's parents' home. From there, the newlyweds embarked on a tireless journey of scientific collaboration, which eventually brought them enormous prestige.

By 1897, Manya decided to advance her education even more by obtaining her doctorate's degree in physics. First, she had to select a new research topic. At that time, the couple had been fascinated by Henri Becquerel's recent discovery of high-energy rays emanating from uranium compounds. Uranium gave off a mysterious energy, which Becquerel noted but had difficulty measuring, and thus he gave up.

Manya picked up where Becquerel left off. Inside a dilapidated shed with no heat, little ventilation, and a leaky roof, Manya toiled away. Soon, she discovered that another element, thorium, also emitted spontaneous rays similar to uranium. Manya named this phenomenon *radioactivity*. As she continued her research, she discovered a mineral called pitchblende that produced stronger radiation than pure uranium. Her logic told her that there must be a new element involved. Excited by the prospect of new discovery, Manya raced back to her makeshift laboratory. Soon, she discovered that pitchblende contained not one, but two radioactive elements. Using chemical analysis, she was able to isolate the first element. "You will have to name it,"[5] Pierre said to his wife. Manya thought of her homeland and suggested, "Could we call it polonium?"[6]

The second element, however, proved to be a much more difficult puzzle to solve. Pierre joined his wife to double her efforts. "In spite of the difficulties of our working conditions, we felt very happy. We lived in our single preoccupation as if in a dream,"[7] Manya said. Finally, after nearly four years of intense labor, radium was discovered. This time their hard work paid off—more than they ever imagined. On December 10, 1903, the Academy of Science of Stockholm announced the winners of the Nobel Prize in physics: one half of the award went to Henri Becquerel, and the other half to Pierre and Manya for their discoveries in radioactivity. In addition to gaining world recognition and fame, Manya and Pierre took home seventy thousand gold francs, a huge sum of money at that time.

Manya went on to receive a second Nobel Prize in chemistry in 1911. She was the first person to win two Nobel Prizes. Who was this famous scientist?

Marie Curie

Marie Curie's immense work on radioactivity led to the treatment of cancer using radiation. It was her sheer determination and diligence that turned a simple curiosity into many brilliant discoveries.

Marie Curie's Bio

Birth Name: Maria "Manya" Sklodowska
Birthplace: Warsaw, Poland
Birth Date: November 7, 1867
Died: July 4, 1934
Age: Sixty-six years old

Achievements and Awards

1903:   Received Doctor of Science degree and the Nobel Prize in Physics

1906:   Became professor of general physics at the University of Paris, the first woman to hold this position

1911:   Received the Nobel Prize in Chemistry

1914:   Appointed director of the Curie Laboratory in the Radium Institute of the University of Paris, founded in 1914

Selected Quotes by Marie Curie

"Be less curious about people and more curious about ideas."

"Life is not easy for any of us. But what of that? We must have perseverance and above all confidence in ourselves. We must believe that we are gifted for something and that this thing must be attained."

"Nothing in life is to be feared, it is only to be understood. Now is the time to understand more, so that we may fear less."

"I was taught that the way of progress is neither swift nor easy."

"I never see what has been done; I only see what remains to be done."

"All my life through, the new sights of nature made me rejoice like a child."

"You cannot hope to build a better world without improving the individuals. To that end, each of us must work for his own improvement, and at the same time share a general responsibility for all humanity, our particular duty being to aid those to whom we think we can be most useful."

"I am among those who think that science has great beauty. A scientist in his laboratory is not only a technician: he is also a child placed before natural phenomena which impress him like a fairy tale."

"I am one of those who think like Nobel, that humanity will draw more good than evil from new discoveries."

"We must not forget that when radium was discovered no one knew that it would prove useful in hospitals. The work was one of pure science. And this is a proof that scientific work must not be considered from the point of view of the direct usefulness of it. It must be done for itself, for the beauty of science, and then there is always the chance that a scientific discovery may become like the radium a benefit for humanity."

Further Reading

Madame Curie: A Biography by Eve Curie
Madame Curie, Daughter of Poland by Robert Woznicki
Grand Obsession: Madame Curie and Her World by Rosalyn Pflaum
Obsessive Genius: The Inner World of Marie Curie by Barbara Goldsmith

REBEL WITH A CAUSE

Cesar was deeply influenced by his mother's stories and use of proverbs. "It takes two to fight, and one can't do it alone,"[1] she often repeated to teach her son about violence. Lessons in charity and generosity were equally emphasized. "You always have to help the needy, and God will help you,"[2] Mom reiterated. Cesar recalled, "If we had an apple or a tiny piece of candy, we had to cut it into five pieces."[3] That was Cesar's education at home.

Before each school day, Cesar had to spend several hours taking care of the animals on the farm and getting water from a nearby river. But that wasn't the hard part. When he got to school, if he didn't speak English, the teacher would smack the ruler right on his knuckles. This was Cesar's first taste of racial discrimination. More would follow. But first he would have to deal with new hardships. Unlike most families, Cesar's family was able to cope with the Great Depression for a number of years by living off the family farm in Arizona. But even they couldn't escape the hard times for long.

By the time Cesar was ten years old, property taxes on the farm mounted to more than four thousand dollars. The family didn't have any money, so they had to forfeit the farm. They were now homeless and broke. So, the family packed the car and left for California with only forty dollars from selling the family cow and some chickens. They didn't have a destination. They were just hoping to settle somewhere in California where there were jobs.

Cesar and his family were now migrant workers desperately looking for work. After driving from one farm to the next, they finally found work: picking peas. After two hours of back-breaking work, the whole family earned only twenty cents. Every day they drove around in search of work. There were so many farm workers looking for jobs that on some days they found a few hours of work while other times went idle. Even worse, the housing cost more than the family income.

After a week or so, with little money left, the family headed north to San Jose to pick cherries. The little money they made after two weeks in the cherry orchards was barely enough to pay for beans, gasoline, and rent. After the cherry harvest, the family found work cutting and pitting apricots. Then it was off to Oxnard to pick walnuts. Dad would be exhausted each time after shaking every limb of the walnut trees.

By the end of the walnut harvest, there was no place to go. It was winter, when the weather got cold and wet. Luckily, a lady they met at the walnut orchards allowed them to put up a tent behind her house. But the little tent on puddles of water was too small to fit everyone. So, Cesar, his brother, and his cousin made their own tent using four long sticks and a canvas on top. In spite of these conditions, Mom insisted that the boys attend school even if they had to wear unmatched socks. On weekends, the boys would huddle up, shivering inside their tent while Mom washed the only sweatshirt each one had.

For years, the family migrated from one job to the next trying to survive with little money, food, and unsanitary living conditions. Somehow, amidst the poverty, the racial discrimination, and the innumerable school transfers, Cesar managed to graduate from eighth grade. But that was as far as he got. After his dad got into a car accident, Cesar had to work full time.

Over the years, his family would drive up and down California picking the crops that were in harvest. Some jobs were easier than others. For Cesar, the worst was pulling sugar beets out of the ground. Some of the beets weighed as much as fifteen pounds and were deeply rooted in a wet, heavy soil like clay. "My hand would split between the thumb and index finger as I pulled, and the stooping also was really painful,"[4] Cesar said.

After that, he told his dad, "I've had it!" and went to join the Navy. But he would regret this decision. In the Navy, he encountered more harassment and racial discrimination. "Those two years were the worst of my life … It's worse than being in prison,"[5] he said. After his military service, Cesar returned home and married his sweetheart in 1948.

Financially, Cesar was still trapped in poverty. Then things slowly began to change. It all started when Cesar met Father McDonnell. The two quickly became friends over long talks about the plight of the migrant workers. Soon, Cesar learned a great deal about the produce growers' use of various unlawful tactics to exploit the farm workers. He began to understand both sides of the struggle but he didn't know how to fight the injustice.

Father McDonnell pointed the way by lending him a few books that would change his life. After reading about Gandhi and his teachings, he had found his answers. But he didn't know how to apply Gandhi's ideas. That's when fate stepped in. A social activist and organizer by the name of Fred Ross came to town searching for a leader to help the migrant workers. He eventually convinced Cesar to become his disciple by clearly explaining how poor people could be united to build a strong power base to fight the growers.

Cesar found his calling in community service. At first, Cesar joined the Community Service Organization (CSO) as a volunteer. Because of his diligence and dedication, the CSO put him on the payroll for thirty-five dollars a week. No longer did he have to worry about financial support for his growing family. By 1962, Cesar was earning one hundred fifty dollars per week at the CSO. This salary was enough to support his wife and eight children.

But something inside him didn't feel right. Cesar felt that more should be done to help improve the farm workers' working conditions. Most farm workers didn't get breaks, fresh water to drink, or have access to portable toilets. The worst part was that the farm workers had to use a short-handled hoe, which forced them to constantly bend over to do their job. So, when the CSO refused to organize a farm workers' union at his request, Cesar resigned and decided to organize one himself.

He knew that the formation of a farm workers' union would be an insurmountable task. The few unions that were established quickly got crushed by the growers. That was because the power of the growers was backed by the police, the courts, state and federal laws, banks, and big corporations. But he was unfazed because he had his wife by his side. "I'm willing to stick it out for ten years and really give it a trial. If it doesn't work, we can figure out something else,"[6] she supported. So, on September 30, 1962, the thirty-five-year-old activist, with the help of Dolores Huerta, established the National Farmworkers Association (NFWA), financed with twelve hundred dollars from his family's life savings.

Tremendous challenges and sacrifices lay ahead. In the beginning, Cesar worked tirelessly to recruit new members, often going without food. Gradually, by teaching and applying Gandhi's nonviolent ideas, Cesar gained the trust of his union members and attracted many new ones. As the union grew, Cesar gained more courage and showed his followers how to strike, walk the picket lines, and march in protest. The growers retaliated with violent and deadly tactics. But each time a protester was injured, beaten, shot, or killed, Cesar urged his followers to stay the course and not fight back. To strengthen morale and draw more attention to his movement, known as the Cause, Cesar fasted for twenty-five days on separate occasions. It worked. Finally, in 1970, after five years of boycotting, the grape growers agreed to sign union contracts. For the first time, working conditions for the migrant workers were improving!

Today, the union now called the United Farm Workers is still fighting for better treatment. Who was this organizer who stood up for the farm workers?

Richard Lam

Cesar Chavez

Cesar Chavez once said "We can turn the world if we can do it nonviolently." He proved that anything is possible if one is willing to sacrifice oneself for the right cause.

Cesar Chavez's Bio

Birth Name: Cesar Estrada Chavez
Birthplace: Yuma, Arizona, United States
Birth Date: March 31, 1927
Died: April 23, 1993
Age: Sixty-six years old

Achievements and Awards

1962:   Founded the United Farm Workers union

1972:   Fasted for twenty-five days in protest of a new Arizona law banning the right of farm workers to strike, boycott, or organize

1988:   At age sixty-one, fasted for thirty-six days to call attention to the harmful effects of pesticides on farm workers and their children

1992:   Led grape workers on walkouts in the Coachella and San Joaquin valleys of California. This resulted in the first pay increase for the grape workers in eight years.

His birthday, March 31, is celebrated in California as a state holiday.

On December 6, 2006, Cesar Chavez was inducted into the California Hall of Fame.

Selected Quotes by Cesar Chavez

"I like the whole idea of sacrifice to do things. If they are done that way, they are more lasting. If they cost more, then we will value them more."

"I am convinced that the truest act of courage, the strongest act of manliness is to sacrifice ourselves for others in a totally nonviolent struggle for justice. To be a man is to suffer for others."

"If you're outraged at conditions, then you can't possibly be free or happy until you devote all your time to changing them and do nothing but that."

"I am positive nonviolence is the way, morally and tactically, especially in our society where those in power resort to clubs, tear gas, and guns."

"There is so much human potential wasted by poverty, so many children forced to quit school to go to work."

"If we get full of anger, we can't think. If we can't think, we can't strategize, and if we can't strategize, we can't win."

"We can turn the world if we can do it nonviolently."

"One of our most powerful nonviolent weapons is the economic boycott."

"There's something about a march that is very powerful. It's a powerful weapon, a powerful organizing tool, and it has a powerful influence on those who participate."

"You are never strong enough that you don't need help."

"When we are really honest with ourselves we must admit that our lives are all that really belong to us. So, it's how we use our lives that determines what kind of men we are. It is my deepest belief that only by giving our lives do we find life."

"There are many reasons for why a man does what he does. To be himself he must be able to give it all. If a leader cannot give it all he cannot expect his people to give anything."

"There is no such thing as defeat in nonviolence."

"Nonviolence is not inaction. It is not discussion. It is not for the timid or weak ... Nonviolence is hard work. It is the willingness to sacrifice. It is the patience to win."

"Those who are willing to sacrifice and be of service have very little difficulty with people. They know what they are all about. People can't help but want to be near them. They help them; they work with them. That's what love is all about. It starts with your heart and radiates out."

FURTHER READING

Cesar Chavez: Autobiography of La Causa by Jacques E. Levy
The Fight in the Fields: Cesar Chavez and the Farmworkers Movement by Susan Ferriss
Remembering Cesar: The Legacy of Cesar Chavez by Ann McGregor

YOU NEVER KNOW

When Althea was young, teachers tried to change her aggressive and defiant attitude by spanking her in class. But that only created more problems. She stopped going to school and played hooky with her girlfriends instead. When Dad found out about her unexcused absences, Althea got a good whipping. After a while, Dad realized that punishment was pointless. "I would just sit there and look at him,"[1] Althea said.

Althea's mischievous behavior went from bad to worse. She got involved in fights with girls and boys, but she always managed to hold her own. Her worst troubles started when she graduated from junior high school. Tired of Yorkville Trade School, she became delinquent for weeks at a time. She would hide in friends' houses or sit by herself in movie theaters during the daytime. And if she didn't have a place to sleep, she would just ride the subway all night long. So, it wasn't long before she dropped out of Yorkville and began hopping from one job to the next to support herself.

When Althea got fired from her last job, two women from the welfare department picked her up as she wandered the streets. They gave the juvenile delinquent two choices: either go to a reformatory or move into a foster home. She chose the foster home. The welfare ladies gave her an allowance while she looked for a new job. But instead of job searching, she went to the movies and played in the streets.

In those days, certain streets in Harlem in New York City were closed to traffic during the daytime so that local residents could use it as a playground. Paddle tennis was very popular on these playgrounds. Althea spent a great deal of time playing this racket sport. Over time, she developed into a fine paddle tennis player and became the champion of her block.

Her superb play eventually caught the eye of a neighbor by the name of Buddy Walker. One day, Buddy purchased two used tennis rackets for Althea and explained to her the benefits of tennis. "You can meet a better class of people and possibly become somebody,"[2] he said. Althea liked the idea and agreed to play a match against one of his friends. Despite her inexperience, Althea played well enough to impress a spectator, Juan Serrell, who was a member of the private Cosmopolitan Tennis Club. Juan then arranged a match for Althea against Fred Johnson, the teaching pro at the club. At the end of the match, the club members decided to pitch in and sponsor Althea for lessons. This was summer 1941.

Fred worked on her tennis game and her attitude. "After a while I began to understand that you could walk out on the court like a lady, be polite to everybody, and still play like a tiger,"[3] Althea said. After a year of lessons, she entered her first tournament and won. That same year, Althea entered the American Tennis Association (ATA) national girls' championship, losing in the finals. After winning the girls' singles title in 1944 and 1945, the eighteen-year-old competed for the women's singles title the following year but lost in the finals. At the end of the match, the ATA members who showed up to watch the match became so disgusted with her cocky attitude that they gave up on her. "I was a pretty dejected kid for a while,"[4] Althea recalled.

However, the feeling of rejection didn't last very long. Her talents on display that day caught the attention of two physicians. Soon after, they suggested to Althea to go to college to get an education and improve her tennis game. But little did they know about Althea's poor school record. When they found out, Dr. Hubert A. Eaton and Dr. Robert W. Johnson came up with a new plan that Althea couldn't refuse. Dr. Eaton would provide room and board for Althea to attend high school and practice tennis with him during the school year. In the summer, she would join Dr. Johnson to compete in tournaments.

Even though Althea had earned only enough credits to enter the seventh grade, the high school where she applied for admission gave her a chance and put her in tenth grade. "That meant I would be able to earn my diploma in three years, and I was determined to do it. I buckled down to my schoolwork like nobody's business,"[5] Althea said.

By summer 1947, she entered nine tournaments and won them all. She was simply the best female tennis player—in Negro tennis. At that time, Althea was prohibited from competition with white women. Finally, at the urging of the ATA, the United States Ladies Tennis

Association (USLTA) opened its doors for Althea to compete in a few small tournaments but not the larger, most prestigious ones.

By June 1949, Althea's diligence paid off as she graduated tenth in her class and accepted an athletic scholarship to Florida A&M University. There, she continued to dominate her tennis rivals. Still, the USLTA refused to admit Althea to the big tournaments. Then out of nowhere, an editorial appeared in a tennis magazine criticizing the USLTA's racist policy. Alice Marble, who was one of the greatest white tennis players in the U.S. at the time, protested, "If Althea represents a challenge to the present crop of women players, it's only fair that they should meet the challenge on the courts where tennis is played. I know those girls, and I can't think of one who would refuse to meet her in competition."[6] Almost overnight, the USLTA reversed its policy and allowed Althea to compete in all of the tournaments.

In the beginning, Althea faced hostile crowds who didn't want to see her play. During one tournament, a spectator kept shouting, "Knock her out of there!"[7] Although it was difficult to play under these harsh conditions, Althea always gave her best effort and never blamed anyone for her losses. Outside the courts, she faced racial discrimination, especially in the South. But that didn't bother her. Slowly, she won the admiration of the spectators with her brilliant display of power, athleticism, and shot-making. But winning against her top opponents proved more difficult. "Whatever it was, the years 1951, '52, and '53 were mostly disappointing for me,"[8] Althea said.

She had yet to win a major tournament. To make things worse, there was constant pressure from the media. An article in *Jet* magazine labeled her "The Biggest Disappointment in Tennis." Althea thought about giving up tennis and joining the Women's Army Corps. But a Harlem tennis instructor, Sydney Llewellyn, urged her to keep playing. "You got a great future in front of you,"[9] he said.

Sidney coached her on better technique and tactics, and helped her gain more self-confidence. Althea listened and practiced day after day. Her hard work finally paid off. On July 7, 1957, she beat Darlene Hard easily, 6-3, 6-2, to become the first black woman to win Wimbledon, the most prestigious tennis tournament in the world. As her name was called to receive her trophy, Althea stepped forward, made a curtsy, and shook hands with the queen of England.

She went on to win the U.S. championship in September 1957 and became the number one player in the world. Who was this female tennis player who broke the color barrier?

Althea Gibson's Bio

Birth Name: Althea Gibson
Birthplace: Silver, South Carolina, United States
Birth Date: August 25, 1927
Died: September 28, 2003
Age: Seventy-six years old

Achievements and Awards

1956:   Won the French championship

1957:   Won Wimbledon and U.S. championship at Forest Hills, New York

1958:   Won Wimbledon and U.S. championship at Forest Hills, New York

1971:   Induction to the International Tennis Hall of Fame

She won a total of fifty-six tournaments, including five major singles titles.

Selected Quotes by Althea Gibson

"I always wanted to be somebody. If I made it, it's half because I was game enough to take a lot of punishment along the way and half because there were a lot of people who cared enough to help me."

"If I am a worthy person, and if I have something worthwhile to contribute, I will be accepted on my own merits, and that is the way I want it."

"I don't consciously beat the drums for any special cause, not even the cause of the Negro in the United States, because I feel that our best chance to advance is to prove ourselves as individuals. That way, when you are accepted, you are accepted voluntarily, because people appreciate you and respect you and want you."

"Not many people, I've found out, find fault with a winner."

Further Reading

I Always Wanted to Be Somebody by Althea Gibson
So Much to Live For by Althea Gibson
Born to Win: The Authorized Biography of Althea Gibson by Frances Clayton Gray

It Was All Worth It

Frank desperately wanted to escape. But he was mired in farm work for his first twenty-one years in Jefferson County, northern New York.

The beginning of each autumn was always a trying experience. He and his little brother, Charles, would get up at five-thirty in the morning when there would be a white frost on the ground and they had to go on barefoot to tend the cows. "In late October, we would pick up potatoes until our backs ached and our fingers were encrusted with dirt and numb with cold,"[1] Charles recalled.

Frank grew up to be tall and lanky but never that sturdy. However, he compensated for whatever physical deficiencies he had with intelligence and persistence. As the years passed, Frank would be occupied with only two things: farm work and schooling. By the time he was sixteen, schooling was over and full-time work on the farm began. This transition did not go over very well with Frank.

His mother knew that he was not cut out to work on the farm. So, she saved enough money to send Frank to take two short business courses at a college in Watertown. Upon completion, he went job searching but had no luck. He returned home dejected. What Frank didn't know was that economic times were extremely tough during the period after the Civil War. Finally, he settled on working for free to gain experience at a small general store under Daniel McNeil.

Not long after, in March 1873, Frank was offered eighteen dollars a month with room and board to work on his Uncle Albon's farm. This was a generous offer, and his father thought he should take it. But Frank's heart was in business, never in farm work. So, he pleaded for a little more time before making such an important decision. Once again, Mom was on his side.

Right after, Frank explained the situation to Daniel McNeil and sought his help. One night, Daniel came back from Watertown with great news. There is an opening at the general store of Augsbury & Moore. The next morning Frank hurried off to apply for the job. At the store was William H. Moore, who promptly put the young man through a series of hard questions.

Finally, Moore said: "If we take you on, you'll have to do all the mean work in the store, deliver packages, wash windows, get down early and sweep the floor, do all the cleaning and any other dirty work that needs to be done. It will be the hardest work you ever did in your life."[2]

"I guess I can do it, sir," replied Frank. "What are you going to pay me?"[3]

"Pay you?" Moore exclaimed. "Why, you ought to pay us for teaching you the business!"[4]

Disheartened, Frank asked, "How long would I have to work for nothing?"[5]

"At least six months,"[6] declared Moore.

Frank quickly came up with a compromise. "I'll work the first three months for nothing," he said, "if you will pay me three dollars and fifty cents a week for the second three months."[7] It was a deal.

For a while, Frank was doing all the dirty work as was expected. Then one day, Moore ordered him to wash all the goods behind the front windows and reorganize them. Frank saw this as a promotion and worked past midnight as he repositioned the goods over and over until the window displays were picture perfect. Moore was impressed. From then on, it was Frank's responsibility to do the window dressings.

By summer 1875, he was working twelve hours a day and earning six dollars a week. With this pay raise, Frank was able to repay his mother for the tuition and afford a nice hat and even a new violin. It was during this time that he fell in love with a young Canadian woman named Jennie Creighton who frequented the store for sewing supplies.

That September, Frank went to work for Moore's competitor, Bushnell, who agreed to pay him ten dollars a week. Bushnell thought he was getting a good salesman, but Frank was not it. So, Bushnell reduced Frank's pay to eight dollars. Frank was so depressed that he wrote a despondent letter to his mother. In response, she offered these encouraging words: "Someday, my son, you will be a rich man."[8]

He worked harder and harder until his health finally broke down. Now, he had no choice but to return to the family farm and recuperate.

After fifteen months of recovery from a respiratory illness, he married Jennie in June 1876. The newlyweds were practically penniless, but they were determined to make it. Frank borrowed six hundred dollars and bought a four-acre farm for the two of them. Four months later, Moore wanted to rehire Frank for ten dollars a week.

"Frank, you go back to the store," Jennie said, "and I'll stay here and take care of the chickens until we get a chance to sell."[9] Then in February 1878, tragedy struck. Frank's mother, his most loyal supporter, died at the age of forty-seven. Overwhelmed with grief, he returned to work. But business was extremely slow, so his boss tried a new sales pitch. Following the suggestion of a former employee, Moore ordered one hundred dollars worth of low-priced merchandise. Frank arranged the new merchandise, which consisted of soap, combs, safety pins, stationery, and other little things on two homemade counters sitting end to end in the middle aisle of the store. Above these two counters was a large sign that read: *ANY ARTICLE ON THIS COUNTER FIVE CENTS*. By the end of day, the five-cent counters were practically cleaned out. After that, Moore invested another hundred dollars.

Frank saw this as a new business idea and a great opportunity. He immediately wanted to open a five-cent store. But he lacked the capital. When he approached his Uncle Albon for money, the uncle flatly refused, saying that his idea was just nonsense. But Frank didn't give up. He had tenacity. Finally, his boss came through and loaned him three hundred dollars to open his store in Utica, Pennsylvania, in 1879.

Sales started off strong, but business began to drop off unexpectedly. After four months, Frank had to close up shop. But he didn't quit. He was convinced that the idea of a discount store was here to stay, not just a fad, as his critics called it. He figured out why his first store failed. It was in a bad location and had a small variety of goods to choose from. After carefully choosing his next location in Lancaster, Pennsylvania, Frank secured a second loan from Moore and ordered a larger variety of goods that included ten-cent items. This store was a success from opening day on June 21, 1879. But he was not content. He wanted a chain of Five-and-Ten stores.

The road to expansion was difficult. Between 1879 and 1886, six of his first twelve stores failed. But that didn't stop him from expanding. He continued to open new stores. By 1911, he had 318 stores. By 1919, Frank owned over one thousand. His assets were worth more than sixty million dollars. Mother was right all along.

Who was this persistent retail store pioneer?

FRANK WOOLWORTH

The simplest ideas are the best ideas, and that's what makes them great. But to take a simple idea and make it work requires hard work and tenacity. Frank Woolworth demonstrated just that.

Frank Woolworth's Bio

Birth Name:	Frank Winfield Woolworth
Birthplace:	Rodman, New York, United States
Birth Date:	April 13, 1852
Died:	April 8, 1919
Age:	Sixty-six years old

Achievements

In 1913, Woolworth built the world's tallest building in New York City. The Woolworth Building cost $13.5 million, which he paid in cash. The skyscraper held the record as the world's tallest building from 1913 to 1930.

Richard Lam

Selected Quotes by Frank Woolworth

"Dreaming never hurt anybody if he keeps working right behind the dream."

"No man can make a success of a business which he does not like."

"Never be afraid to run. If your business isn't going ahead right, back out and take a fresh start."

"A business is like a snowball: one man can easily push it along for awhile but the snowball becomes so large if pushed ahead that help must be obtained to roll it—and if you don't keep rolling it, it will soon melt."

"No business can stand stationary for any considerable period. It either rises or falls and, if left to itself, the tendency is for it to fall."

"I put it down to the great buying power that allows us to drive prices lower by helping factories to make their goods more cheaply. And to making sure that everyone rich or poor is welcomed in and treated with the same respect."

Further Reading

Remembering Woolworth's: A Nostalgic History of the World's Most Famous Five-and-Dime by Karen Plunkett Powell
Five and Ten: The Fabulous Life of F. W. Woolworth by John K. Winkler
Skyline Queen and the Merchant Prince: The Woolworth Story by John P. Nichols

NEVER OUT OF STYLE

Gabrielle was born in the poorhouse in Saumur, a small town along the Loire River in France. Throughout her childhood, her family migrated from one place to another following Dad as he went in search of work. Sometimes Dad disappeared, leaving the family alone to fend for itself.

By the time Gabrielle was eleven years old, her mother's health had deteriorated after many years of living on the road in poverty while trying to raise five children almost single-handedly. In the middle of the winter in 1895, Mom died. Dad was nowhere to be found. A week after his wife died, he dropped off his three daughters at the orphanage run by nuns at Aubazine and disappeared for good. Gabrielle's two younger brothers were taken in by a farm household who promised them room and board in exchange for child labor.

For the next six years, Gabrielle and her two sisters, Julie and Antoinette, spent the majority of the time at the convent where they endured many cold nights without heat. Seeing that Gabrielle was a quick learner, the nuns taught her how to sew. During the holidays, the three sisters paid visits to their grandparents and Aunt Louise. As a seamstress, Aunt Louise inspired Gabrielle by showing her how to sew and decorate hats with an artistic flair. Gabrielle learned how to embellish a blouse and use leftover pieces of cloth for collars.

By the time Gabrielle was eighteen, she was asked to leave Aubazine. Because she had no intentions of becoming a nun, Gabrielle was sent to a boarding school where young women were trained to be housewives. Soon, she was hired as a shop assistant at a lingerie and hosiery shop. Her reputation as a fine seamstress quickly spread. Women specifically asked Gabrielle to do their wardrobe alterations. Some customers took their alterations directly to her apartment.

During the next few years, she pursued a few other interests, including a career in theater. But her singing and dancing skills were inadequate. In August 1908, Gabrielle turned twenty-five and was unsure where her life was heading. Most women at her age would have married, but Gabrielle was different. She didn't want to be forever dependent on men and their money. When an older gentleman by the name of Jacques Balsan suggested that she marry his younger brother, Etienne, Gabrielle brushed him aside.

"I don't love him,"[1] she refused.

"You'll end up in the dumps. What will happen to you?"[2] he worried.

"I don't know and I don't care. I want to work,"[3] she objected.

"Work! You don't know anything,"[4] he insulted.

Gabrielle didn't respond.

Jacques was wrong. She knew one thing. More and more fashion-minded women were interested in her hats. They wanted to know where she bought them. This gave her an idea. She bought simple, flat-topped straw-hats or boaters by the dozen from a department store and trimmed them with ribbons and lace in her unique style similar to the way Aunt Louise showed her. Then she turned around and sold the hats to fashionably-conscious women who wore them as the latest fashion.

The popular demand of her hats gave Gabrielle another idea. She convinced her boyfriend, Arthur Capel, to lend her money to open a shop. She was no longer just a seamstress but also a milliner, one who designs and sells hats for women. Her loyal and wealthy clients who liked her hats so much encouraged her to broaden her fashion line. Shortly thereafter, knitted shirts, sweaters, and blazers designed in her unique style were on display.

With her growing success, she began to see a career in fashion. Even though she didn't possess any drawing skills, she had an eye for detail. She could tell what made her clients look good with just one simple glance and then quickly make the necessary alterations. By summer 1913, Gabrielle had opened a second fashion house in Deauville, the English Channel resort, and introduced turtleneck sweaters. Two years later, Gabrielle opened Biarritz's first fashion house. She had sixty girls sewing under her. By early 1916, the combined staff in Paris, Deauville, and Biarritz totaled three hundred. Business was so good that Gabrielle was able to repay all the money to Arthur.

Then, suddenly tragedy struck. Arthur Capel died in a car crash. "I lost everything when I lost Capel,"[5] Gabrielle mourned. To relieve her pain and suffering, she returned to what she did best. By now, her fashion and her name were synonymous with high culture and exquisite taste. Women quickly adopted her latest trend. When she introduced her "little black dress," women had worn black only at funerals but Gabrielle made it fashionable to wear it anytime. She convinced wealthy women to put on slacks for comfort and ease of movement when participating in sports or other leisure activities.

One day, Gabrielle decided to add a perfume to her name. Until 1920, perfumes smelled like flowers. Gabrielle wanted to change all that. "I don't want hints of roses, of lilies of the valley," she told Ernest Beaux, a perfume maker, "I want a perfume that is composed."[6]

Gabrielle spent long days in the lab studying the perfume-making process. At the end, Beaux concocted seven or eight samples. She sniffed them all then came back to sample number five. "That's what I expected," she said. "A perfume unlike any other ever made. A woman's perfume, redolent, evocative of woman."[7] But there was a slight problem. The chosen sample would be very expensive to make because it contained more than eighty ingredients, including the pricey jasmine. "In that case, put even more jasmine in it,"[8] she said. "I want to make it the world's most expensive perfume."[9]

To advertise her new perfume, she had her salesgirls spray the fitting rooms with the new scent. Women began asking about the new perfume. A few weeks later, the first commercial launch of the perfume became an instant hit. Gabrielle's perfume and couture was the most expensive in Paris. But by 1931, the fashion industry was struggling. Europe was facing tough economic times. The few wealthy women who remained wore plain dresses, sweaters, and slacks like everyone else. Washable fabrics like cotton replaced the more expensive fabrics. In her 1931 spring collection, Gabrielle presented thirty-five different cotton evening dresses, and she began to use zippers to reduce costs. To bring back the customers, Gabrielle cut her prices in half. But even that didn't work.

After Hitler invaded Poland, she closed all her fashion houses and went into retirement. She thought the world no longer cared about fashion. But she was wrong. After Gabrielle closed her shops, more and more men entered the fashion industry. By 1947, a forty-two-year-old newcomer named Christian Dior had revolutionized women's fashion with his latest creations. Women's fashion now belonged to Dior and his male contemporaries. This didn't sit well with Gabrielle. She always believed that women were better fashion designers for women.

After fifteen years of enjoying a life of leisure, at the age of seventy, Gabrielle came out of retirement. She sensed the time was right to bring back her classic line with a little refinement. On February 5, 1954, she premiered with 130 models showing off her new collection. After the show, the fashion critics made a quick exit for the doors. The reviews were devastating. A magazine criticized, "From the first dress, we knew that the style belonged to the past."[10] She was disappointed but didn't give up. When her business partner, Pierre Wertheimer, went to see her, he found her working on her next collection. "You know I want to go on, go on and win,"[11] she told him. "You're right," he said. "You're right to go on."[12] Three weeks later, *Life* magazine from America wrote, "The name behind the most famous perfume in the world never lost her touch."[13] Once again, Gabrielle was on top of the fashion world.

Today, her name remains a luxury brand in the fashion world. Who was this famous trendsetter?

Gabrielle Chanel

Gabrielle Chanel always seemed to know what women wanted to wear. But it was always her courage to try new ideas that set the latest fashion trend. On the road to success, courage and persistence never go out of style.

Gabrielle Chanel's Bio

Birth Name: Gabrielle Bonheur "Coco" Chanel
Birthplace: Saumur, France
Birth Date: August 19, 1883
Died: January 10, 1971
Age: Eighty-seven years old

Achievements

She took what were considered poor fabrics like cotton and jersey and popularized their use in the fashion industry.

Chanel No. 5 was Gabrielle's first perfume introduced in 1921. She was the first person to put a designer's name on a bottle of fragrance. Since its introduction, many other designers have followed suit.

Selected Quotes by Gabrielle Chanel

"If you were born without wings, do nothing to prevent their growing."

"To earn a living in the feminine trade you must know women."

"Fashion is not something that exists in dresses only: fashion is something in the air. It's the wind that blows in the new fashion; you feel it coming, you smell it. Fashion is in the sky, in the street, fashion has to do with ideas, the way we live, what is happening."

"A beautiful dress may look beautiful on a hanger, but that means nothing. It must be seen on the shoulders, with the movement of the arms, the legs, and the waist."

"Fashion does not exist unless it goes down into the streets. The fashion that remains in the salons has no more significance than a costume ball."

"Make the dress first, not the embellishment."

"Comfort has forms. Love has colors. A skirt is made for crossing the legs and an armhole for crossing the arms."

"To disguise oneself is charming: to have oneself disguised is sad."

"The time comes when one can do nothing further to a work; this is when it has reached its worst."

"A failed innovation is painful: revival of it is sinister."

"One can get used to ugliness, but never to negligence."

"Luxury is a necessity that begins where necessity ends."

FURTHER READING

Gabrielle: A Woman of Her Own by Axel Madsen
Mademoiselle Chanel by Pierre Galante
Gabrielle and Her World: Friends, Fashion, and Fame by Edmonde
Charles Roux

FREEDOM FIGHTER

It took some time for Rolihlahla to live up to the meaning of his name, "troublemaker."

As a child, he spent most of his time playing with other boys in his village of Qunu. By age five, he was herding sheep and calves. His education came from his mother, who enchanted him with stories handed down from past generations. "These tales stimulated my childish imagination, and usually contained some moral lesson,"[1] Rolihlahla recalled.

No one in his family had ever attended school until one day a family friend approached his mother. "Your son is a clever young fellow," he said. "He should go to school."[2] Mom passed the advice to Dad, who then agreed that his seven-year-old son should be educated. Dad took Rolihlahla aside and dressed him properly for school. "My father took a pair of his trousers and cut them at the knee. Then he took a piece of string and cinched the trousers at the waist,"[3] he said. Until that time, Rolihlahla always wore a blanket that covered one shoulder and was pinned at the waist.

Two years later, Rolihlahla's life took a drastic turn. The nine-year-old boy saw his father pass away at home. After a brief period of mourning, Mom took Rolihlahla to Mqhekezweni, where the Paramount Chief Jongintaba Dalindyebo had offered to become the guardian of the boy. As Mom departed, she turned to her son and said, "Brace yourself, my boy!"[4]

Rolihlahla quickly settled in his new home. "Although I missed Qunu and my mother, I was completely absorbed in my new world,"[5] he said. He worked hard in school where he studied English, Xhosa, history, and geography. "I did well in school not so much through cleverness as through doggedness,"[6] he said. The chief had often told him, "It is not for you to spend your life mining the white man's gold, never knowing how to write your name."[7]

Big plans laid ahead for the young Rolihlahla. The chief wanted him to be educated and become a counselor. After completing his primary education at a local mission school, he arrived at the Clarkebury Boarding Institute, where he completed his junior certificate in two years instead of the usual three. When he finished his secondary education at Healdtown, he enrolled at the University College of Fort Hare, where he was later elected to the Student Representative Council (SRC). The same day as the election, Rolihlahla submitted his resignation because he had decided to boycott the elections along with the vast majority of the student body. Most of the students felt the SRC had too limited influence on university affairs.

When the principal threatened Rolihlahla with expulsion for not rejoining the SRC, Rolihlahla stood firm by his convictions. "I knew it was foolhardy for me to leave Fort Hare, but at the moment I needed to compromise, I simply could not do so,"[8] he said. So, he gave up his college career and returned to Mqhekezweni. The chief was incensed by his actions and mandated that he return to school in the fall. A few weeks later, the chief informed Rolihlahla and his cousin, Justice, that they were to be married immediately. The brides had already been selected and cattle were given to the families of the brides as bride-price. The two young men were shocked and speechless. Neither of them believed in arranged marriages, so they took matters into their own hands.

They ran away to the city of Johannesburg, South Africa. There, Rolihlahla was introduced to Walter Sisulu, who was a successful realtor and a prominent local leader in the black community. Walter was impressed by his courageous act at Fort Hare and his ambition to become a lawyer. An arrangement was made where Rolihlahla would work as a clerk for Lazar Sidelsky and resume his college studies through correspondence courses. Mr. Sidelsky was a white lawyer who supported blacks. "He was a patient and generous teacher and sought to impart not only the details of the law but the philosophy behind it,"[9] Rolihlahla said.

In the beginning, life in the big city was difficult. The salary of two pounds a week from the law firm was barely enough to survive. Often, Rolihlahla went hungry and without a change of clothes. He walked twelve miles to town and back so that he could save money for candles, which were used for late-night studies. To make matters worse, he had to face racial discrimination.

In August 1943, Rolihlahla took a path that forever changed his life. He marched with ten thousand people in support of a bus boycott. After nine days, the bus company canceled the fare hike. Rolihlahla was impressed by the effectiveness of the boycott—but Mr. Sidelsky was not. Time and time again, he warned Rolihlahla for getting involved in politics. "If you get into politics," he said, "your practice will suffer. You will get into trouble with the authorities who are often your allies in your work. You will lose all your clients, you will go bankrupt, you will break up your family, and you will end up in jail."[10]

Rolihlahla was undaunted. Instead, he followed Walter Sisulu's footsteps and joined the African National Congress (ANC) in 1943. The ANC was formed in 1912 to bring all Africans together as one people to defend their rights and freedoms against the oppressive white government that had been in power for centuries. A group of young Africans became dissatisfied with the lack of progress made by the senior leaders of the ANC. So, under the leadership of Anton Lembede, Rohlihlahla, Walter, and a number of others, they came together to found the African National Congress Youth League in September 1944.

The Youth League decided that more aggressive measures were needed to get the government's attention. They adopted Gandhi's ideas of nonviolent resistance mass movement, which had already been proven to be highly effective. By 1948, the new government under the leadership of Daniel Malan adopted a much more abusive policy: apartheid. Under apartheid, which means apartness, each racial group (blacks, whites, coloreds, and Indians) were geographically separated from one another. It was a crime to enter places reserved for "whites only," such as government buildings, hospitals, restaurants, parks, beaches, and restrooms.

With the passing of each new law, the white government tightened its control over the nonwhite population and increased its abusive power. As president of the Youth League, Rolihlahla discreetly traveled the country organizing people to fight the injustice. Not long after, he was arrested and banned from traveling and attending gatherings. But this didn't stop him. He often disguised himself as a chauffeur to evade police and continued his work. As time went on, the government grew more and more impatient and crushed peaceful demonstrations with brutality, which often resulted in killings. This left the ANC with no other choice but to prepare for an armed struggle.

Rolihlahla took charge of a new organization known as MK to come up with tactics that would punish the government. Later, he was arrested with ten others and charged with sabotage. During the eight-month hearing known as the Rivonia Trial, Rolihlahla defended his own actions. "I have cherished the ideal of a democratic and free society in which all persons live together in harmony and with equal opportunities. It is an ideal which I hope to live for and to achieve. But if needs be, it is an ideal for which I am prepared to die,"[11] he said. In the end, the verdict was life imprisonment on Robben Island, where he was forced to do hard labor. While in prison, his son and mother died. His wife was frequently harassed and sometimes banned from the biannual visitations.

The ANC was banned, and violence between the blacks and whites ravaged the country. Several times, the government offered Rolihlahla release from prison in exchange for renouncing the violence. But he flatly refused. "Prisoners cannot enter into contracts—only free men can negotiate,"[12] he said. Finally, a compromise was made with President F. W. de Klerk, and Rolihlahla was freed after twenty-seven years in prison. After intense negotiations over three and a half years, apartheid officially came to an end on April 27, 1994, when South Africa held its first multiracial election.

Rolihlahla became the first black president of South Africa. Who was this freedom fighter?

NELSON MANDELA

Nelson Mandela always fought for what was right and just no matter how many or how difficult the sacrifices that had to be made.

Nelson Mandela's Bio

Birth Name:	Nelson Rolihlahla Mandela
Birthplace:	Mvezo, Eastern Cape, South Africa
Birth Date:	July 18, 1918
Died:	
Age:	Ninety years old

Achievements and Awards

Received Nobel Peace Prize in 1993

Mandela served twenty-seven years in prison, spending eighteen of those years on Robben Island.

Rolihlahla Mandela became the first member of his family to attend school, where his teacher, Miss Mdingane, gave him the English name "Nelson."

Mandela, as leader of the ANC, was inaugurated on May 10, 1994, as South Africa's first black president.

Selected Quotes by Nelson Mandela

"We must use time wisely and forever realize that the time is always ripe to do right."

"I learned that courage was not the absence of fear, but the triumph over it. The brave man is not he who does not feel afraid, but he who conquers that fear."

"It always seems impossible until it's done."

"A good head and a good heart are always a formidable combination."

"Education is the most powerful weapon which you can use to change the world."

"If you talk to a man in a language he understands, that goes to his head. If you talk to him in his language, that goes to his heart."

"If you want to make peace with your enemy, you have to work with your enemy. Then he becomes your partner."

"It is better to lead from behind and to put others in front, especially when you celebrate victory when nice things occur. You take the front line when there is danger. Then people will appreciate your leadership."

"There is no passion to be found playing small—in settling for a life that is less than the one you are capable of living."

"The greatest glory in living lies not in never falling, but in rising every time we fall."

"Man's goodness is a flame that can be hidden but never extinguished."

"Virtue and generosity will be rewarded in ways that one cannot know."

Further Reading

Nelson Mandela: The Struggle Is My Life by Nelson Mandela
Long Walk to Freedom: The Autobiography of Nelson Mandela by Nelson Mandela
Mandela: The Authorized Biography by Anthony Sampson

Dare to Soar

Mary was a tomboy.

"I was fond of basketball, bicycling, tennis, and I tried any and all strenuous games,"[1] she said. Not to mention, she rode horses without a saddle. But these activities were rather harmless compared to the others. Whenever Mary jumped the fence surrounding her house coming home from school, Grandma had to remind her about the etiquette ladies needed to exercise. Then Grandpa had to confiscate the little .22 rifle that Mary and her younger sister used for blowing up bottles off the back fence.

The family moved around quite a bit in the Midwest as her father searched unsuccessfully for a stable job. As a result, Mary never stayed at the same school for long. The summer before she entered the seventh grade, her father took her to the Iowa State Fair, where she saw her first airplane. She was not impressed. "It was a thing of rusty wire and wood and looked not at all interesting,"[2] she remembered.

As the growing years passed, somehow Mary was able to graduate in the usual four years' time from Hyde Park High School in Chicago after having gone to six high schools. After graduation, she waited around a year and then entered junior college at the Ogontz School near Philadelphia. During winter break of her senior year, she went to Toronto, Canada, to visit her sister. There she witnessed for the first time the atrocities of the First World War when four one-legged men walked past her.

"Mother, I'd like to stay here and help in the hospitals," Mary said. "I can't bear the thought of going back to school and being so useless."[3]

"That means giving up graduating,"[4] said Mom.

Mary didn't care. "I gave up all thought of returning to school and took steps to become a nurse's aide,"[5] she recalled. After spending months in Toronto working in a hospital until the war ended, Mary became interested in medicine. But after a few months at Columbia University, she left New York and headed out west to pursue medical research instead. When she got to California, her interest changed once again.

This time it was aviation. The more air shows she saw, the more interested she became. One day, Dad took her to Rogers Field near Los Angeles and bought her a ticket for a ride with pilot Frank Hawks. "As soon as we left the ground," Mary said, "I knew I had to fly."[6] When she told her parents about her new passion, neither had any objections. Within a few days she signed up for lessons and went home asking for money. "You really weren't serious, were you?"[7] Dad asked surprisingly. "I thought you were just wishing. I can't afford to let you have instruction,"[8] he added. Undeterred, Mary found her first job at a telephone company to pay for the lessons.

"I want to fly," she told Neta Snook, the female flight instructor, "and I understand you take students."[9] Neta took her under her wings. From then on, Mary occupied all of her time with work during the weekdays and flying lessons on the weekends. After a year, she received her pilot's license. Although she enjoyed flying and doing aerial stunts, the thought of making a living as a pilot never crossed her mind.

After a year or so of working various odd jobs, she decided to return east and settled for social work at the Denison House in Boston. There, she worked long hours helping the needy and spent her free time flying with the local pilots. "It was sheer fun," Mary said, "And it did keep me in touch with flying."[10] Then a phone call changed her life.

One afternoon in April 1928, Captain H. H. Railey telephoned Mary at the Denison House. Reluctant to take the call at first, Mary then listened and learned that a woman had planned to make a transatlantic flight, but she had changed her mind. Now, she wanted an American woman to be the first woman to cross the Atlantic. "Would you like to fly the Atlantic?"[11] he asked. "Yes," she said promptly. This was an adventure of a lifetime that she could not pass up.

Joined by pilot Bill Stultz and mechanic Louis E. Gordon, the team took off from Trepassey Bay, Newfoundland, on June 17, 1928, and landed at Burry Port, Wales, after twenty hours and forty minutes. News of this milestone quickly spread throughout the world.

Celebrations and invitations were bestowed upon the crew in London, and when they returned home they were given a ticker-tape parade in New York City.

This historic flight brought immense publicity for Mary in particular. Her publicist and book publisher, George P. Putnam, immediately capitalized on Mary's new fame. First, George got Mary to write a book, and then he had her tour the country to boost book sales. It wasn't too long before Mary was making a good living from endorsements, book royalties, a magazine column, and lectures. In six months, she had traveled across the country and back, visited dozens of cities, and given countless speeches and interviews. For the first time in her life, she believed it might be possible to earn a decent living as an aviatrix.

A year later in the summer of 1929, Mary took part in the Cleveland Women's Air Derby, a cross-country race in which she came in third place. It was during this time that George began courting Mary. After six proposals, Mary finally agreed and the couple was married on February 7, 1931.

Always wanting to push her limit, she decided to set another milestone. On a January morning in 1932, Mary asked her husband, "Would you mind if I flew the Atlantic?"[12] George got excited. Both knew all about the dangers. At that time, only a man by the name of Charles Lindbergh had flown solo across the Atlantic. Two adventurers who had tried it never made it back. But Mary believed in herself. "I chose to fly the Atlantic because I wanted to. It was in a measure, a self-justification—a proving to me, and to anyone else interested, that a woman with adequate experience could do it,"[13] she said.

On May 19, at 7:12 PM, Mary took off from Harbor Grace, Newfoundland. Four hours into the flight, Mary's plane encountered mechanical problems. Her altimeter stopped working. She had to guess how high or low she was flying in the dark sky. For more than an hour, she fought against Mother Nature as high winds, thunder, and lightning tried to knock her off course. Later, her fuel gauge malfunctioned, leaving her clueless as to how much fuel remained. Finally, after fifteen hours, she crossed the vast ocean and landed on a pasture in Londonderry, Ireland. This achievement brought Mary even greater world fame.

Still, she wanted to achieve more. In 1935, she became the first person to fly solo across the Pacific Ocean from Hawaii to California. Later that year, Mary set another record by flying solo from Mexico City, Mexico, to Newark, New Jersey. But she wasn't done yet. "I have a feeling there is just one more flight in my system ... this trip around the world is it,"[14] she said. At age thirty-nine, she soared into aviation history and became a legend.

Richard Lam

Who was this courageous aviatrix?

AMELIA EARHART

Amelia Earhart did what she wanted to do. It was always her great courage that took her to new heights. She set many aviation records in her time, at a time when men dominated the field.

Amelia Earhart's Bio

Birth Name:	Amelia Mary Earhart
Birthplace:	Atchison, Kansas, United States
Birth Date:	July 24, 1897
Died:	July 2, 1937
Age:	Thirty-nine years old

Achievements

1921: Began flying lessons
Bought first plane

1922: Broke women's altitude record at fourteen thousand feet

1928: First woman to fly across the Atlantic

1932: First woman to fly solo across the Atlantic

1933: First woman to fly solo non-stop coast–to-coast across the United States

1935: First person to fly solo across the Pacific Ocean between Honolulu, Hawaii, and Oakland, California

SELECTED QUOTES BY AMELIA EARHART

"I knew I had to fly."

"I want to do it because I want to do it. Women must try to do things as men have tried. When they fail, their failure must be but a challenge to others."

"The most difficult thing is the decision to act, the rest is merely tenacity. The fears are paper tigers. You can do anything you decide to do. You can act to change and control your life; and the procedure, the process is its own reward."

"The woman who can create her own job is the woman who will win fame and fortune."

"The most effective way to do it, is to do it."

"My ambition is to have this wonderful gift produce practical results for the future of commercial flying and for the women who may want to fly tomorrow's planes."

"Preparation, I have often said, is rightly two-thirds of any venture."

"It usually works out that if one follows where an interest leads, the knowledge or contacts somehow or other will be found useful sometime. To the person who has learned to swim well comes the opportunity to rescue a drowning man."

"To want in one's head to do a thing, for its own sake; to enjoy doing it; to concentrate all of one's energies upon it—that is not only the surest guarantee of its success. It is also being true to oneself."

FURTHER READING

Amelia Earhart: A Biography by Doris L. Rich
Ameila Earhart: The Sky's No Limit by Lori Van Pelt
The Fun of It: Random Records of My Flying and of Women in Aviation
by Amelia Earhart

Mr. Perseverance

"I do the very best I know how—the very best I can; and I mean to keep doing so until the end." That he did. No matter what the obstacles or challenges were, somehow he managed to overcome them all.

Life would test this man very early. He nearly drowned when he was six years old. Three years later, his mother died after drinking the milk from the family cow, which had eaten a poisonous weed. She was only thirty-four years old. Many years later he recalled, "In this sad world of ours, sorrow comes to all; and to the young it comes with bitterest agony, because it takes them unawares."[1]

The loss of the caregiver left all the household responsibilities to his older sister, Sarah. A year later, their father brought much-needed help when he married Sarah Bush Johnston, a widow with three young children. Seeing the untidy place, this sweet and energetic woman got to work right away. Sally, as she was called, brought motherly love and tender care back into the little home. Although she couldn't read or write, she knew the value of education. A special bond quickly developed between her and her stepson.

She saw the intelligent child's thirst for learning. "He read all the books he could lay his hands on," Sally said, "and when he came across a passage that struck him, he would write it down on boards. If he had no paper, he kept it there until he got paper—then he would rewrite it."[2] Sally never let the children bother him. She always told the other children that he was going to be a great man someday.

In those days, in the 1800s, there weren't many schools. He had to walk four miles to school when it was in session. But poverty cut short his formal education. "All my schooling did not amount to one year,"[3] he said. Nevertheless, he continued to learn, on his own. "The things I want to know are in books; my best friend is the man who'll get me a book I haven't read,"[4] he said. Too poor to buy books, he satisfied his hunger for learning by borrowing them from neighbors and strangers. One fall afternoon, he walked nearly twenty miles to borrow a book from a lawyer. From his neighbors, he borrowed and read *Aesop's Fables,* Parson Weem's *The Life of George Washington,* and a few others. When rain soaked Weem's biography, he confessed to Josiah Crawford and then pulled every ear of corn from Josiah's fields for three days to pay for the book.

As the teenage years passed, he grew into a strong and tall young man. By seventeen, he was able to cut down timbers and split logs easily with his ax. No matter what job he was engaged in, he always saved time for learning. He would either read a book or be engaged in something educational. On a number of occasions, he walked fifteen miles to a courthouse to observe how lawyers speak, argue, and conduct themselves. He mimicked the way political speakers influenced the crowd.

For the next couple of years, he settled on a routine of working odd jobs and learning from borrowed books. Then tragedy struck. In January 1828, when he was almost nineteen, his sister died during childbirth. After three long months, his somber mood began to lighten up when he accepted the job to help navigate a flatboat loaded with produce down the Mississippi River to New Orleans. Three months later, he returned home with twenty-five dollars in hand and turned it over to his father. Later, he worked at a general store under a fellow named Denton Offutt. Soon, his reputation was the talk of the town. Once, he walked six miles to pay back a few cents to a woman who overpaid. And when he gave a woman four ounces of tea instead of the eight that was paid for, he hiked miles to deliver the remainder.

Unfortunately, within a few months, Offutt's store failed and he was out of a job. Shortly after, he purchased a chain of failing grocery stores with a fellow named William F. Berry hoping to turn a profit. At the same time, the election for state legislators was approaching. So, he decided to enter the race. With the aid of Mentor Graham, the local schoolteacher, he spent weeks working on his first public address to announce his candidacy for the state legislature. Not surprisingly, the young, inexperienced politician lost in August 1832.

Another failure soon followed. In a matter of months, the grocery stores were out of business. Both men were unqualified to be merchants. His partner was busy drinking whisky while he was busy reading books.

His streak of bad luck finally stopped in May 1833. He was appointed postmaster of his small town in New Salem, Illinois. This part-time job didn't pay much, but it allowed him the benefit of reading all the newspapers for free. A few months later, a friend offered him the job of assistant surveyor. This was a highly technical job that required a good deal of mathematics and surveying, which he lacked. But this didn't stop him. Under the tutelage of Mentor Graham once again, in six weeks, he had mastered the necessary knowledge in geometry, trigonometry, and surveying to begin work. His surveys were so accurate and detailed that he was called on to settle boundary disputes.

Two years after his first running for political office, he ran again for the state legislature and won. Now at age twenty-five, he had won his first important political office, with better pay than ever. A prominent lawyer by the name of John Todd Stuart urged him to study law by lending him his law books. He took his advice and studied the law books with the usual diligence. When Mentor Graham suggested that he improve his grammar, he immediately took off to track down a copy of *Kirkham's Grammar* from a farmer living six miles away. Many years later, after having taught more than five thousand students, Mentor Graham said that he was the "most studious, diligent, straightforward young man in the pursuit of knowledge and literature" he had ever met. "I have known him," said the schoolteacher, "to study for hours the best way of three to express an idea."[5]

Just when things were going well, he encountered another string of bad luck. First, his former business partner, Berry, died unexpectedly in January 1835, leaving him the joint debt of eleven hundred dollars from their business failure. Then his fiancée, Ann Rutledge, died of typhoid seven months later. This ordeal nearly destroyed him. In the weeks that followed, he wouldn't eat and he couldn't sleep. His friends took his pocket-knife away and kept a watchful eye on him after he threatened to kill himself. He would walk five miles to Ann's grave and stay there for so long that his friend would get worried and go and bring him home. His close friend, Bowling Greene, and his wife took him under their care, and gradually he recovered.

Slowly, his luck began to turn around. He was re-elected to the state legislature in 1836. Then he passed his law exams and got his license. The next year he left New Salem for good as he rode into the new capital Springfield, Illinois on a borrowed horse to try practicing law. There, he joined John Todd Stuart's law firm. Business was extremely slow during the first six months. He had only five small clients. He became so discouraged that he confessed to a local carpenter one day that he was thinking about quitting law practice and going into carpentry instead. But he didn't quit. Soon, his honest reputation spread, and business gradually improved. One time, a client sent him a check for twenty-five dollars to write a lease. He replied, "Fifteen dollars is enough for the job. I send you a receipt for fifteen dollars and return to you a ten-dollar bill."[6]

At the age of thirty-three, he finally settled down and married. His law practice was now a success, but his heart was still in politics. So, he ran for Congress in February 1843 but was defeated. Tragedy struck again in February 1850. His four-year-old son, Edward, died. He ran for the United States Senate and was defeated in 1855. It was the same result in 1858. But despite the defeat, his name was being mentioned for the presidency. To this, he replied, "I must, in candor, say I do not think myself fit for the presidency."[7] But he never gave up. By early autumn 1859, he decided to run again. Finally, after numerous defeats, he had achieved his greatest victory. But before he moved to the White House, he made one last visit to see his old stepmother.

Richard Lam

He became one of the greatest American heroes. Who was he?

ABRAHAM LINCOLN

On March 4, 1861, Abraham Lincoln became the sixteenth president of the United States. The life of Abraham Lincoln is a lesson that demonstrates the value of determination and perseverance.

ABRAHAM LINCOLN'S BIO

Birth Name:	Abraham Lincoln
Birthplace:	Hardin County, Kentucky, United States
Birth Date:	February 12, 1809
Died:	April 15, 1865
Age:	Fifty-six years old

ACHIEVEMENTS

On September 22, 1862, he announced the Emancipation Proclamation which by law freed the slaves. Lincoln later said: "I never, in my life, felt more certain that I was doing right, than I do in signing this paper."

On November 19, 1863, he gave the famous Gettysburg Address beginning with the familiar phrase, "Four scores and seven years ago …"

Richard Lam

Selected Quotes by Abraham Lincoln

"I do the very best I know how—the very best I can; and I mean to keep doing so until the end. If the end brings me out all right, what's said against me won't amount to anything. If the end brings me out wrong, ten angels swearing I was right would make no difference."

"Leave nothing for tomorrow which can be done today."

"Get the books, and read and study them till you understand them in their principal features; and that is the main thing ... Your own resolution to succeed is more important than any other one thing."

"I will prepare and some day my chance will come."

"Things may come to those who wait, but only the things left by those who hustle."

"It's not the years in your life that matter, it's the life in your years."

"Whatever you are, be a good one."

"When I do good, I feel good; when I do bad, I feel bad, and that is my religion."

"Discourage litigation. Persuade your neighbors to compromise whenever you can. Point out to them how the nominal winner is often a real loser—in fees, expenses, and waste of time. As a peacemaker the lawyer has a superior opportunity of being a good man. There will still be business enough."

"Stand with anybody that stands *right*. Stand with him while he is right and *part* with him when he goes wrong."

"I know not how to aid you, save in the assurance of one of mature age, and much severe experience, that you cannot fail, if you resolutely determine, that you will not."

218

"Adhere to your purpose and you will soon feel as well as you ever did. On the contrary, if you falter, and give up, you will lose the power of keeping any resolution, and will regret it all your life."

"If you would win a man to your cause, first convince him that you are his sincere friend."

"You may deceive all the people part of the time, and part of the people all the time, but not all the people all the time."

"Character is like a tree and reputation like its shadow. The shadow is what we think of it; the tree is the real thing."

"I will study and get ready, and perhaps my chance will come."

"I don't like that man. I must get to know him better."

"I am for those means which will give the greatest good to the greatest number."

FURTHER READING

Lincoln the Unknown by Dale Carnegie
Abraham Lincoln, His Story in His Own Words by Ralph Geoffrey
Abraham Lincoln: The Prairie Years and the War Years by Carl Sandburg

Endnotes

Change the World

1. Smaridge, *The Light Within*, 23.
2. Ibid., 32.
3. Ibid., 33.
4. Ibid., 48.
5. Ibid., 48.
6. Standing, *Maria Montessori*, 32.
7. Ibid., 38.

The Young Man and the Sea

1. Eunson, *The Pearl King*, 31.
2. Ibid., 77.
3. Ibid., 81.
4. Ibid., 84.
5. Ibid., 91.
6. Ibid., 91.
7. Ibid., 95.
8. Ibid., 95.
9. Ibid., 98.
10. Ibid., 106.

Shooting Star

1. Swartwout, *Missie*, 26.
2. Riley, *The Life and Legacy*, 12.
3. Swartwout, *Missie*, 52.
4. Ibid., 52.

Peace by Peace

1. Gandhi, *Gandhi: An Autobiography*, 20.
2. Ibid., 6.
3. Ibid., 27.
4. Ibid., 27.
5. Ibid., 87.
6. Ibid., 94.
7. Ibid., 112.
8. Ibid., 112.
9. Ibid., 134.

Iron Will

1. Wilson, *I Will Be Doctor!*, 15.
2. Ibid., 51.
3. Ibid., 51.
4. Blackwell, *Pioneer Work in Opening*, 27.
5. Ibid., 29.
6. Ibid., 29.

Dreams Do Come True

1. Watts, *The Magic Kingdom*, 59.
2. Barrier, *The Animated Man*, 19.
3. Mosley, *Disney's World*, 70.
4. Ibid., 70.
5. Ibid., 71.
6. Ibid., 99.
7. Greene, *The Man Behind the Magic*, 5.
8. Ibid., 5.

The Pursuit of Happiness

1. Clinton, *Harriet Tubman*, 18.
2. Larson, *Bound For The Promised Land*, 40.
3. Ibid., 42.
4. Ibid., 84.

5. Ibid., 88.
6. Clinton, *Harriet Tubman*, 91.

Al Mighty

1. Clark, *Edison*, 9.
2. Josephson, *Edison*, 24.
3. Ibid., 24.
4. Ibid., 33.
5. Ibid., 178.
6. Bureau of International Information Programs, "Thomas A. Edison," U. S. Department of State, http://usinfo.org/enus/life/people/edison.html (accessed June 16, 2009).
7. Clark, *Edison*, 97.
8. Ibid., 97.

Heart of Gold

1. Spink, *Mother Teresa*, 7.
2. Chawla, *Mother Teresa*, 3.
3. Spink, *Mother Teresa*, 19.
4. Ibid., 19.
5. Ibid., 22.
6. Chawla, *Mother Teresa*, 20.
7. Spink, *Mother Teresa*, 32.
8. Ibid., 37.
9. Ibid., 298.
10. Ibid., 298.
11. Ibid., 298.

Stand and Deliver

1. King, *The Autobiography*, 7.
2. Ibid., 7.
3. Ibid., 10.
4. Ibid., 16.
5. Ibid., 16.
6. Ibid., 55.

7. Ibid., 58.
8. Ibid., 86.
9. Ibid., 37.

Let Your Voice Be Heard

1. Stevenson, *Marian Anderson*, 66.
2. Ibid., 67.
3. Ibid., 67.
4. Ibid., 69.
5. Anderson, *My Lord, What a Morning*, 38.
6. Ibid., 38.
7. Newman, *Marian Anderson*, 25.
8. Stevenson, *Marian Anderson*, 91.
9. Newman, *Marian Anderson*, 27.
10. Anderson, *My Lord, What a Morning*, 73.
11. Newman, *Marian Anderson*, 43.
12. Ibid., 43.
13. Anderson, *My Lord, What a Morning*, 145.

Follow Your Passion

1. Huffington, *Picasso*, 23.
2. Ibid., 23.
3. Ibid., 27.
4. Ibid., 28.
5. Ibid., 38.
6. Ibid., 38.
7. Mailer, *Portrait of Picasso*, 5.

Have No Fear

1. Freedman, *Eleanor Roosevelt*, 2.
2. Roosevelt, *The Autobiography of Eleanor Roosevelt*, 411.
3. Ibid., 5.
4. Ibid., 10.
5. Ibid., 24.
6. Freedman, *Eleanor Roosevelt*, 78.

7. Ibid., 98.
8. Ibid., 111.
9. Ibid., 111.
10. Roosevelt, *The Autobiography of Eleanor Roosevelt*, 412.

Golden Opportunities

1. Kroc, *Grinding It Out*, 15.
2. Ibid., 15.
3. Ibid., 15.
4. Ibid., 15.
5. Ibid., 15.
6. Ibid., 56.
7. Ibid., 56.
8. Ibid., 13.

No Matter What They Say

1. Ogden, *Maggie*, 36.
2. Ibid., 36.
3. Thatcher, *Margaret Thatcher*, 19.
4. Ibid., 5.
5. Ibid., 32.
6. Ibid., 28.
7. Ibid., 39.
8. Ibid., 67.
9. Ibid., 71.
10. Ibid., 79.
11. Ibid., 94.
12. Ibid., 96.
13. Ogden, *Maggie*, 112.
14. Ibid., 112.
15. Ibid., 112.

Climb as High as You Can

1. Hillary, *Nothing Venture, Nothing Win*, 18.
2. Ibid., 19.

3. Ibid., 20.
4. Ibid., 22.
5. Ibid., 24.
6. Ibid., 28.
7. Ibid., 30.
8. Ibid., 40.
9. Ibid., 78.

Always Be Curious

1. Curie, *Madame Curie*, 57.
2. Ibid., 57.
3. Ibid., 57–58.
4. Ibid., 72.
5. Ibid., 161.
6. Ibid., 161.
7. Ibid., 170–71.

Rebel With a Cause

1. Levy, *Cesar Chavez*, 18.
2. Ibid., 70.
3. Ibid., 19.
4. Ibid., 73.
5. Ibid., 84.
6. Ibid., 5.

You Never Know

1. Gibson, *I Always Wanted to be Somebody*, 17.
2. Ibid., 34.
3. Ibid., 35.
4. Ibid., 43.
5. Ibid., 49.
6. Ibid., 67–68.
7. Ibid., 76.
8. Ibid., 81.
9. Ibid., 89.

It Was All Worth It

1. Winkler, *Five and Ten*, 4.
2. Ibid., 11.
3. Ibid., 11.
4. Ibid., 12.
5. Ibid., 12.
6. Ibid., 12.
7. Ibid., 12.
8. Ibid., 18.
9. Ibid., 22.

Never Out of Style

1. Madsen, *Chanel*, 44.
2. Ibid., 45.
3. Ibid., 45.
4. Ibid., 45.
5. Ibid., 105.
6. Ibid., 134.
7. Ibid., 135.
8. Ibid., 135.
9. Ibid., 135.
10. Ibid., 288.
11. Ibid., 289.
12. Ibid., 289.
13. Ibid., 290.

Freedom Fighter

1. Mandela, *Long Walk to Freedom*, 10.
2. Ibid., 12.
3. Ibid., 12.
4. Ibid., 15.
5. Ibid., 15.
6. Ibid., 15.
7. Ibid., 27.
8. Ibid., 45.

9. Ibid., 64.
10. Ibid., 76.
11. Mandela, *The Struggle is My Life*, 9.
12. Ibid., 196.

Dare to Soar

1. Earhart, *The Fun of It*, 8.
2. Rich, *Amelia Earhart*, 9.
3. Earhart, *The Fun of It*, 19.
4. Ibid., 19.
5. Ibid., 19.
6. Rich, *Amelia Earhart*, 24.
7. Earhart, *The Fun of It*, 25.
8. Ibid., 25.
9. Rich, *Amelia Earhart*, 27.
10. Earhart, *The Fun of It*, 57.
11. Ibid., 59.
12. Rich, *Amelia Earhart*, 129.
13. Earhart, *The Fun of It*, 210.
14. Rich, *Amelia Earhart*, 257.

Mr. Perseverance

1. Philips, *Abraham Lincoln*, 4.
2. Ibid., 6.
3. Sandburg, *Abraham Lincoln*, 13.
4. Ibid., 13.
5. Carnegie, *Lincoln: The Unknown*, 43.
6. Sandburg, *Abraham Lincoln*, 127.
7. North, *Abe Lincoln*, 134.

Bibliography

Anderson, Marian. *My Lord, What a Morning: An Autobiography*. New York: Viking, 1956.

Barrier, Michael. *The Animated Man: A Life of Walt Disney*. Berkeley and Los Angeles, California: University of California Press, 2007.

Black, Allida M. *Courage in a Dangerous World: The Political Writings of Eleanor Roosevelt*. New York: Columbia University Press, 1999.

Blackwell, Elizabeth. *Pioneer Work in Opening the Medical Profession to Women*. New York: Schocken Books, 1977.

Bureau of International Information Programs. "Thomas A. Edison," U. S. Department of State. http://usinfo.org/enus/life/people/edison.html.

Carnegie, Dale. *Lincoln the Unknown*. Garden City, New York: Dale Carnegie & Associates, Inc., 1932.

Charles Roux, Edmonde. *Gabrielle and Her World: Friends, Fashion, and Fame*. New York: Vendome Press, 2005.

Chawla, Navin. *Mother Teresa: The Authorized Biography*. Rockport, Massachusetts: Element Books, 1996.

Clark, Ronald W. *Edison: The Man Who Made the Future*. New York: Putnam, 1977.

Clinton, Catherine. *Harriet Tubman: The Road to Freedom*. Boston, Massachusetts: Little, Brown, 2004.

Conot, Robert E. *A Streak of Luck*. New York: Da Capo Press, 1979.

Curie, Eve. *Madame Curie: A Biography*. Garden City, New York: Doubleday, Doran, 1939.

Earhart, Amelia. *The Fun of It: Random Records of My Flying and of Women in Aviation*. Chicago: Academy Press, 1977.

Easwaran, Eknath. *Gandhi, The Man: The Story of His Transformation*. Tomales, California: Nilgiri Press, 1997.

Eunson, Robert. *The Pearl King: The Story of the Fabulous Mikimoto*. New York: Greenberg, 1955.

Ferriss, Susan. *The Fight in the Fields: Cesar Chavez and the Farmworkers Movement*. New York: Harcourt Brace, 1998.

Frady, Marshall. *Martin Luther King, Jr.: A Life*. New York: Penguin, 2006.

Freedman, Russell. *Eleanor Roosevelt: A Life of Discovery*. New York: Clarion Books, 1993.

Gabler, Neal. *Walt Disney: The Triumph of the American Imagination*. New York: Knopf, 2006.

Galante, Pierre. *Mademoiselle Chanel*. Chicago: H. Regnery Co., 1973.

Gandhi, Mahatma. *The Essential Writings of Mahatma Gandhi*. Delhi, New York: Oxford University Press, 2005.

Gandhi, Mohandas K. *Autobiography: The Story of My Experiments with Truth*. New York: Dover, 1983.

Geoffrey, Ralph. *Abraham Lincoln, His Story in His Own Words*. Garden City, New York: Doubleday, 1975.

Gibson, Althea. *I Always Wanted to be Somebody*. New York: Harper, 1958.

Gibson, Althea. *So Much to Live For*. New York: Putnam, 1968.

Goldsmith, Barbara. *Obsessive Genius: The Inner World of Marie Curie*. New York: W. W. Norton, 2005.

Gray, Frances Clayton. *Born to Win: The Authorized Biography of Althea Gibson*. Hoboken, New Jersey: John Wiley & Sons, 2004.

Greene, Katherine and Richard Greene. *The Man behind the Magic*. New York: Viking, 1998.

Hillary, Edmund. *Nothing Venture, Nothing Win*. New York: Coward, McCann & Geoghegan, 1975.

Hillary, Edmund. *View from the Summit*. New York: Pocket Books, 2000.

Johnston, Alexa. *Reaching the Summit: Sir Edmund Hillary's Life of Adventure*. New York: DK Publishing, 2005.

Josephson, Mathew. *Edison*. New York: McGraw-Hill, 1959.

Kasper, Shirl. *Annie Oakley*. Norman, Oklahoma: University of Oklahoma Press, 1992.

King, Martin Luther. *The Autobiography of Martin Luther King Jr*. New York: Warner Books, 1998.

King, Martin Luther. *The Martin Luther King, Jr. Companion: Quotations from the Speeches, Essays, and Books of Martin Luther King Jr*. New York: St. Martin's Press, 1993.

Kramer, Rita. *Maria Montessori: A Biography.* Reading, Massachusetts: Addison-Wesley, 1988.

Kroc, Ray. *Grinding It Out: The Making Of McDonald's.* Chicago: H. Regnery, 1977.

Larson, Kate Clifford. *Bound for the Promised Land: Harriet Tubman, Portrait of an American Hero.* New York: One World/Ballantine Books, 2005.

Levy, Jacques E. *Cesar Chavez: Autobiography of La Causa.* New York: Norton, 1975.

Love, John F. *McDonald's: Behind the Arches.* Toronto, New York: Bantam Books, 1995.

Lowry, Beverly. *Harriet Tubman: Imagining a Life.* New York: Doubleday, 2007.

Madsen, Axel. *Gabrielle: A Woman of Her Own.* New York: H. Holt, 1990.

Mailer, Norman. *Portrait of Picasso as a Young Man.* New York: Atlantic Monthly Press, 1995.

Malvern, Corinne. *The First Woman Doctor: The Story of Elizabeth Blackwell, M.D.* New York: Messner, 1944.

Mandela, Nelson. *Long Walk to Freedom: The Autobiography of Nelson Mandela.* Boston, Massachusetts: Little, Brown, 1994.

Mandela, Nelson. *The Struggle Is My Life.* New York: Pathfinder Press, 1990.

McGregor, Ann. *Remembering Cesar: The Legacy of Cesar Chavez.* Clovis, California: Quill Driver Books, 2000.

Swartwout, Anne Fern. *Missie.* Blanchester, Ohio: Brown Publishing Co., 1947.

Mosley, Leonard. *Disney's World*. New York: Stein and Day, 1985.

Newman, Shirlee P. *Marian Anderson: Lady from Philadelphia*. Philadelphia, Pennsylvannia: Westminister Press, 1965.

Nichols, John P. *Skyline Queen and the Merchant Prince: The Woolworth Story*. New York: Trident Press, 1973.

Ogden, Chris. *Maggie: An Intimate Portrait of a Woman in Power*. New York: Simon and Schuster, 1990.

Pflaum, Rosalynd. *Grand Obsession: Madame Curie and Her World*. New York: Doubleday, 1989.

Powell, Karen Plunkett. *Remembering Woolworth's: A Nostalgic History of the World's Most Famous Five-and-Dime*. New York: St. Martin's Press, 1999.

Rich, Doris L. *Amelia Earhart: A Biography*. Washington, DC: Smithsonian Institution Press, 1989.

Richardson, John. *A Life of Picasso: The Prodigy, 1881–1906*. New York: Knopf, 2007.

Riley, Glenda. *The Life and Legacy of Annie Oakley*. Norman, Oklahoma: University of Oklahoma Press, 1994.

Roosevelt, Eleanor. *The Autobiography of Eleanor Roosevelt*. New York: Da Capo Press, 1992.

Sampson, Anthony. *Mandela: The Authorized Biography*. New York: Knopf, 1999.

Sandburg, Carl. *Abraham Lincoln: The Prairie Years and the War Years*. New York: Harcourt, Brace, 1954.

Smaridge, Norah. *The Light Within: The Story of Maria Montessori.* New York: Hawthorn Books, 1965.

Spink, Kathryn. *Mother Teresa: A Complete Authorized Biography.* San Francisco, California: HarperSanFrancisco, 1997.

Standing E. M. *Maria Montessori: Her Life and Work.* New York: New American Library, 1984.

Stassinopoulos, Arianna. *Picasso: Creator and Destroyer.* New York: Simon and Schuster, 1988.

Stevenson, Janet. *Marian Anderson: Singing to the World.* Chicago: Encyclopedia Britannica Press, 1963.

Teresa. *Mother Teresa: In My Own Words.* Liguori, Missouri: Liguori Publications, 1996.

Thatcher, Margaret. *Margaret Thatcher: The Path to Power.* New York: HarperCollins, 1995.

Thomson, Andrew. *Margaret Thatcher: The Woman Within.* Oxford, England: Clio Press, 1989.

Van Pelt, Lori. *Amelia Earhart: The Sky's No Limit.* New York: Forge, 2005.

Watts, Steven. *The Magic Kingdom.* Boston, Massachusetts: Houghton Mifflin, 1997.

Wilson, Dorothy Clarke. *I Will Be Doctor, The Story of America's First Woman Physician.* Nashville, Tennessee: Abingdon Press, 1983.

Wilson, Dorothy Clarke. *Lone Woman.* Boston, Massachusetts: Little, Brown and Company, 1970.

Winkler, John K. *Five and Ten: The Fabulous Life of F.W. Woolworth.* New York: R. M. McBride & Company, 1940.

Woznicki, Robert. *Madame Curie, Daughter of Poland.* Miami, Florida: American Institute of Polish Culture, 1983.

Made in the USA
Lexington, KY
29 June 2010